THE LAST OF THE EBB

" A vivid narrative of the German push on the Aisne
in May, 1918, by one on the spot "
—*The Financial Times*

" A truly excellent and moving book, in which it
would be difficult to find anything to criticise—either
of matter or manner.   There is also a wealth
of human touches which make this book
attractive to read "
—*Fighting Forces*

" Sidney Rogerson's account of the anxiety and
suspense on the British side, where war-worn and
tired divisions were the only troops available,
is dramatic in the highest degree.   It is
a wonderfully written and compiled book "
—*Tatler*

" He writes very vividly and with abundant details
of a disaster to British arms of which the public
at home heard but little at the time.   It is a record
of defeat, but of honourable defeat "
—*Sheffield Telegraph*

" The writer succeeds in giving a detailed picture
of stirring episodes of which he was a witness "
—*Edinburgh Citizen*

" A brilliant and dramatic record of the crushing
defeat of General Duchêne's army in the
German offensive in May, 1918 "
—*Dorset County Chronicle*

" An excellent account of the battle and
experience by one brigade "
—*Birmingham Post*

" One of the most lucid narratives of modern
warfare . . . an account in stirring language
of incredible personal adventures and experiences
of one who saw fighting in the intensest form
known as the Great War "
—*Manchester Evening Chronicle*

" The writer succeeds in giving a vivid picture of
stirring episodes of which he was a witness "
—*Edinburgh Citizen*

" Taken together these two narratives make an
absorbing and convincing study, and give an
unusually clear picture of an episode of the war "
—*Burton Observer*

THE LAST
OF THE EBB

The Battle of the Aisne, 1918

SIDNEY ROGERSON

Foreword by Peter Rogerson

Introduction by Malcolm Brown

FRONTLINE BOOKS

A Greenhill Book

The Last of the Ebb: The Battle of the Aisne, 1918

A Greenhill Book

This edition published in 2011 by Frontline Books,
an imprint of Pen & Sword Books Limited,
47 Church Street, Barnsley, S. Yorkshire, S70 2AS

ISBN 978-1-84832-611-8

A CIP data record for this title is available from the British Library

PUBLISHING HISTORY
The Last of the Ebb was first published in 1937 by Arthur Barker,
London, and reprinted in 2007 by Greenhill Books with a new
introduction by Malcolm Brown and a new foreword by Peter
Rogerson. This new publication by Frontline Books is the first
paperback edition of the work.

For more information on our books, please visit
www.frontline-books.com, email info@frontline-books.com
or write to us at the above address.

Printed and bound in Great Britain by MPG Books Ltd

CONTENTS

List of Illustrations   vii

Foreword   xiii

Introduction   xix

Author's Introduction   xxxiii

I   The Shrubbery   1

II   The Aisne   19

III   High Ground   37

IV   The Vesle   51

V   The Ridges   63

VI   The Marne   79

VII   The Reckoning   107

The German Side   119
    By Major-General A. D. Von Unruh

ILLUSTRATIONS

(between pages 58–59)

All pictures reproduced courtesy of
The Imperial War Museum

" THERE IS MUCH WIRE "
German trench-mortar team passing the old
8th Division front line near Berry-au-Bac.

" EVERYWHERE WAS RUIN "
Our captured positions on the Aisne Canal seen
from Hill 108.   Berry-au-Bac in the background.

THE BRIDGE AT PONTAVERT
German infantry being ferried across the Aisne.
The vital crossings were seized within three
hours of the opening assault.

GERMAN INFANTRY ADVANCING
ACROSS THE BATTLE ZONE

" BY WAY OF SAVIGNY . . . WE WENT "
French and British troops at Savigny, May 28.
(Note signpost to Jonchery.)

" BY NOW FRENCH AND BRITISH WERE
WELL AND TRULY MIXED UP "

" THEIR INFANTRY SWARMED ACROSS
THE OPEN COUNTRY "
German machine-gun detachment approaching
the River Vesle.

" CRUGNY WAS ALREADY IN GERMAN
HANDS "
German transport approaching Crugny
(in distance).

IN THE OPEN
British infantry awaiting the enemy, May 29.
German infantry in the unspoilt country on
May 27.

" TWO-WAY TRAFFIC CONGESTION
OF THE WORST KIND "
8th Divisional infantry, French infantry, transport,
and cookers at Passy, May 29, 1918.

THEY REMEMBERED 1870.   REFUGEES
CROSSING THE MARNE AT REUIL

REFUGEES AND RETREATING FRENCH
TROOPS AT CHATILLON

THE LAST HANDFUL
8th Divisional infantry crossing the Marne.

PRISONERS
Men of the West Yorkshires being marched
back.   First British prisoners being brought back
through a mine crater.

THE WINTERBERG (CALIFORNIE
PLATEAU) AFTER ITS CAPTURE
F. Marshal von Hindenburg and H.I.M. the
Kaiser on the Winterberg, 28th May.

" THE HEADQUARTERS OF THE 150TH
BRIGADE WERE TAKEN AND THE
BRIGADIER MADE PRISONER "
The Kaiser talking to the captured Brigadier.
With H.I.M. are Generals von Böhn and
von Conta.

Maps

The Battle of the Aisne, 1918.   x–xi

Detail map of French positions and first two
days fighting 8th Division.   7

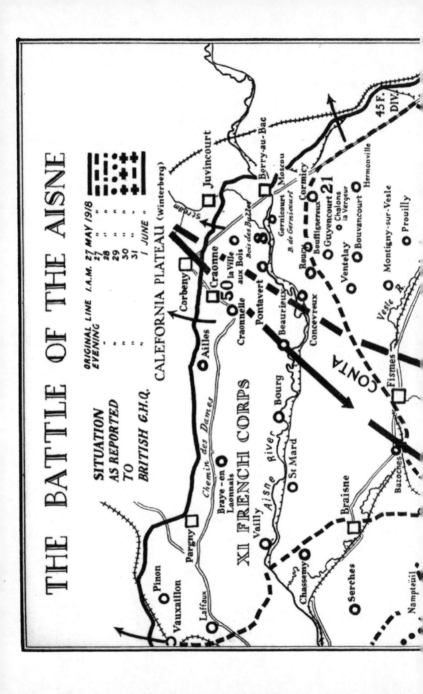

THE BATTLE OF THE AISNE

SITUATION
AS REPORTED
TO
BRITISH G.H.Q.

ORIGINAL LINE I.A.M. 27 MAY 1918
EVENING ...... 27 " "
...... 28 " "
...... 29 " "
...... 30 " "
...... 31 " "
...... 1 JUNE " "

CALEFORNIA PLATEAU (Winterberg)

XI FRENCH CORPS

Chemin des Dames

Aisne River

Vesle R.

CONTA

45 F. DIV.

Pinon
Vauxaillon
Laffaux
Pargny
Braye-en Laonnais
Vailly
Bourg
St Mard
Chassemy
Serches
Braisne
Bazoches
Nampteuil
Ailles
Corbeny
Craonne
Craonnelle
Pontavert
Beaurieux
Concevreux
Fismes
Juvincourt
Berry-au-Bac
Moscou
Cormicy
Hermonville
Gernicourt
B. de Gernicourt
Bois des Buttes
Ville aux Bois
Bourg
Bouffignereux
Guyencourt
Ventelay
Bouvancourt
Chalons la Vergeur
Montigny-sur-Vesle
Prouilly
50
8
21
St Cream

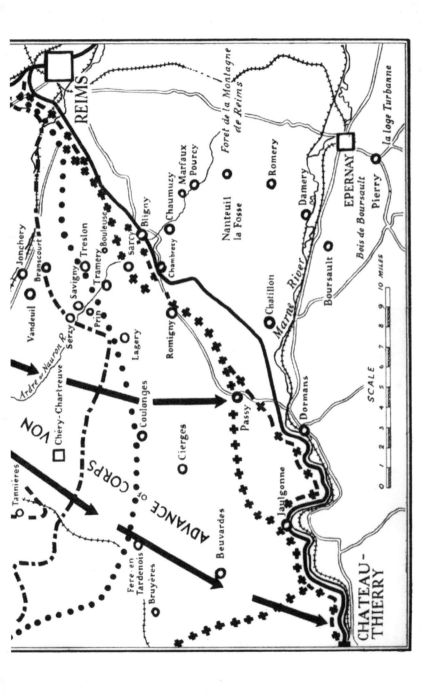

FOREWORD

As a small boy, my bedroom doubled up as my father's dressing room. I would go to bed with his memorabilia looking down upon me. A team photograph of Worksop college 1st XI ; a doctor's wooden medicine chest circa 1850 ; and a First World War German artillery officer's helmet complete with mounted ball on top, and the German Imperial Eagle spread across the front. Along with all my books and toys, they made up the decoration of my room.

When a bit older I asked my father (who was now in his early fifties) about the helmet, he recounted how he had picked it up during the war and that it was worn by an artillery officer, having the ball on top and not the spike of the infantry more often seen in old photographs. This was the first inkling I had of his service for three years during that terrible war. I discovered a little later, in the top drawer of his lovely old oak trouser press on the landing, further pieces of battlefield detritus ; a small bayonet in its scabbard and a piccolo. Other items in the house suddenly made sense. A grim painting in my brother's bedroom depicting a patrol in No-Man's-Land, a waterlogged shell hole with a blasted corpse and, silhouetted against the darkening sky, two helmeted British Tommies. Various highly-polished brass shell cases as door-stops, and a photograph of a distinguished senior army officer, Brigadier James Jack, my father's commanding officer in 1916. I had heard references to " Jolly Jimmy Jack " on numerous occasions and could now put a face to him. Depicted in the first of his two war memoirs *Twelve Days*, he left a lasting impression on my father, who went on to help him publish his war diaries in 1964 in collaboration with John Terraine.

Bit by bit I learned more of my father's wartime exploits but regret, in later life, that I never pushed him to answer any questions on his personal experiences of that time. As a young child I was not really interested and, anyway, I was rather in awe of him and felt it perhaps rather impertinent ! It was made doubly difficult because for all his working life thereafter, in London with ICI, the War Office and the Wellcome Foundation, he only came home to Suffolk at weekends. These days were very precious to him but I never had a real opportunity to get him to reminisce. My mother told me one day that he had been recommended for a M.C. and the D.S.O., the relevance of which meant little to me at the time. So many exploits during that war were deserving of medals. He always looked the " military man ", with his erect posture, barrel chest and neat moustache but was really a countryman with a zest for living and interest in people. He was a fount of knowledge on a whole range of subjects (the diversity of his other books bear testament to this) and was fond of quoting from history or reciting chunks of Latin. His charm and wit made him excellent company.

As the weekend approached, the atmosphere in the household would change to one of excited expectancy as my mother picked him up from Stowmarket station. If he was writing a book, he would be closeted with his papers in his own world of words. Sporadically he would break for a burst of exercise, and any of us children would be summoned to grab the other end of one of his enormous cross-cut saws to do some vigorous sawing of logs, or go " hacking back " the then overgrown garden. One of our favourite times with him would be the afternoon walk, often incorporating a visit to a local church. His twelve Large White breeding sows were his pride and joy, and many visits were made with titbits for them and their families. It was during these weekends that, realising my love of the countryside and farming, he decided to write a book about farming for me called *Both Sides of the Road* which was beautifully illustrated by Charles Tunnicliffe. If there was time on a Sunday evening, he would draw us magical pictures of speeding locomotives or weird imaginary beasts (one of which I had pinned up on the wall of my room at school for years). He was an accomplished artist and but for the war, would have followed this profession.

I had the privilege to serve with my father's old Regiment, The Prince of Wales's Own Regiment of Yorkshire (The West Yorkshire Regiment having amalgamated with The East Yorkshire Regiment in 1958). I very soon read *Twelve Days* and *The Last of the Ebb*, which answered many of my earlier questions and uncertainties. At this time in the early 1960s, some of the senior officers in the 1st Battalion knew of my father and had read his books. A few of the older retired officers could recall his visit to the 1st Battalion the West Yorkshire Regiment in the Canal Zone in Egypt in the early 1950s. At this time he had been seconded to the War Office from ICI to help the Minister for War to promote the Army as an attractive career, having decided to end National Service. He arrived as a VIP and " Old Comrade " and was treated royally. He had little contact with the regiment thereafter until, in the early 1960s, I persuaded him to attend one of our annual Regimental Dinners. I stayed with him in his club and had to put his dress shirt studs in his shirt. He always was very fumble-fingered. At the dinner, after all those years, he was the star attraction and there was much reminiscing of his visit to Egypt. He was the only one wearing First World War medals. While at the War Office one of the CIGSs he advised was Field Marshal Sir William Slim who had himself been a corporal in The West Yorks.

I am glad that my father's books about the First World War are now being made available to a new readership, at a time when interest in that war seems to be increasing year by year.

Twelve Days—retitled as *Twelve Days on the Somme*—appeared under the imprint of Greenhill

Books in 2006 to considerable critical acclaim, and it is especially gratifying to my brother and sister as well as myself that its success has paved the way for the republication of his companion volume about the critical 1918 Battle of the Aisne.   It is our hope this new edition of *The Last of the Ebb*, will meet with a similar welcoming response.

PETER ROGERSON

2007

No-Man's-Land ?   Please can we have our usual war back.

Sidney Rogerson, by this time a brigade staff-officer after long service as an infantry officer and company commander in the line, had a good phrase for what he knew were the expected elements of Western Front warfare : " drab monotony and battle racket ".   But neither of these were evident in the valley of the River Aisne—far to the south of such well-known battle-zones as the Somme, Arras, Loos or Ypres—where he and several thousand other British soldiers unexpectedly found themselves in May 1918.

The sector in question was, as it remains, an area of great natural beauty.   It is a mix of valleys and high ridges, each ridge paler than the last as you look towards them, each valley with its sleepy river, the Aisne itself so languid at certain points it needs a stretch of canal to help it along.   In every direction are well-tilled fields, swathes of lush woodland, and a scatter of grey-stone villages, each with its ancient church and token château.   The area lies within the triangle formed by the cathedral city of Laon to the north, German regional headquarters between 1914 and 1918, Soissons to the south-west, and Rheims (Reims) to the south-east.   A prominent feature is the road striding across the Aisne heights which bears the curious name of the " Chemin des Dames ", the " Road of the Ladies " : a highway constructed in the eighteenth century so that the daughters of King Louis XV—father of the sixteenth of that name who, like his consort Marie Antoinette,

perished in the Place de la Révolution in 1792—
could travel at speed between the palace at
Compiègne and the Château de la Bove, the
residence of a highly-favoured member of the royal
circle, the Duchess of Nemours.

The Chemin des Dames, however, was more than
just a geographical curiosity. It had become a
serious bone of contention, being in part occupied
by the Allies and in part by the Germans. In April
1917 the flamboyant glib-talking French general,
Robert Nivelle, who had come well out of the final
phase of the Battle of Verdun, had flung his forces
over the Chemin des Dames ridge confident that he
could beat the Germans by a simple mixture of dash
and élan. The result was a catastrophic defeat,
Nivelle's disgrace and the French military mutinies
which would leave a deep wound in the French
national psyche.

By the spring of 1918, however, the area had gone
quiet. There had been, reputedly, a holocaust of
tanks ; but as happened after even such ferocious
killing-matches as the 1916 Battle of the Somme, by
the following year nature had mantled the detritus of
war with tall grass and wild flowers, investing the
former battleground with an impression of rural
calm. Wrote Rogerson :

> Now each shattered tree stump had covered its wounds
> with a wealth of close foliage. In the shell-holes grass
> had grown and water-plants. Near the gun emplace-
> ments in the reserve line grew lilies of the valley,
> forget-me-nots, larkspur, and honey-suckle . . . Among

the reeds of the Aisne River I hunted swallow-tail butterflies and rare Camberwell Beauties, and even found a whitethroat's nest with eggs.

He was not the only writer to comment on the peaceful aspect of the Aisne sector at this time. " In some places in the trenches ", noted the historian of one battalion, " there were arbours covered with rambling roses ", while the C.O. of another told his officers that they were going to trenches which by constant improvement had become " rather like Savoy Hotel removed underground ". The author's fellow staff-officer prominently named in the book, Captain Philip Ledward, found himself billeted in a nearby village in the Curé's house, " where white and purple lilac trees in full flower pushed their branches actually into my bedroom ".

The general " atmosphere of tranquillity ", as Rogerson described it, was emphasized by the prevailing silence, which was only broken by an occasional shell that seemed to arrive " in a leisurely sort of way ... exploding apologetically, without injury to anyone ", serving, if anything, " to increase rather than diminish the general impression that in such a setting hostilities were impossible ".

If this suggested almost an Eden, it was one where, very soon, the serpent would strike. What is more, the battle that was about to take place in this apparently benign setting in the war's final year was no minor sideshow ; rather it was a make-or-break encounter which, had its outcome been different, might have brought that now ancient conflict to a very different ending.

We see 1940 as the year in which Britain came closest to defeat : the year in which France collapsed under the blistering attack of Hitler's powerful *Wehrmacht*, forcing the British to bring their beleaguered expeditionary force home across the English Channel. What is often overlooked, or not even known about, is that its predecessor, the British Expeditionary Force (B.E.F.) of the first war was not far from what might be described as a " Dunkirk situation " in the late spring of 1918. Desperate to force a conclusion before the newly arrived forces of the United States were ready to bring their potentially limitless resources into play, the Germans launched a series of massive offensives in France, the aim of which was to split apart the armies of the British and the French, strike through to the coast and force a quick shock victory. Failing to achieve what they hoped for in March, they tried again in April and then again in May. The May offensive, called by the Germans " Operation Blücher ", pushed the Allied forces to within sixty miles of Paris, brought Germany's biggest weapon of artillery—the Krupp 120 mm cannon " Long Max "—to within shelling distance of the French capital and created such an impact in Britain's government circles that in early June the possibility was seriously discussed in Cabinet of withdrawing the whole British Army from France " if the French cracked ". Anybody interested in the Second World War will recall that it was the fact that the

French " cracked " in 1940 that led to the Dunkirk evacuation. Fortunately they did not crack in 1918. But the situation was as touch and go as that ; defeat, with the ignominy of having to make terms with the German military leadership, was a real possibility.

It is this particular nail-biting crisis which is the subject of Sidney Rogerson's book, and its place in this series of attacks is indicated by his apt title. As he explains in his Introduction, the ebb for one side implies the top of the tide for the other. But once that ebb had been survived, the tide-turn was virtually inevitable. Thereafter the victory, though it would have to be fought for every inch of the way, was virtually assured. But in the crucial period which Rogerson describes, the outcome was far from certain. Indeed, he shows us that now distant war at what was arguably its greatest crunch-point. That this is also a vivid, brilliantly written book only adds to its significance and appeal.

But what were Rogerson and his fellow soldiers in khaki doing in that uncharacteristically beautiful part of the front in May 1918 ?

The fact was that his division, the 8th, together with three other divisions, the 21st, the 25th and the 50th, had suffered so severely in the earlier offensives in March and April, in which the British had taken the brunt and been forced to yield much ground, that they had been withdrawn from the trenches in northern France and moved south to what was assumed to be a quieter part of the line. Having no such areas at their disposal, the British were assigned to a sector under French command.

As Rogerson put it : " We had come down to the French front for a rest-cure. We expected neither to attack nor to be attacked. " This transfer of forces was made easier by the fact that the French and British were now subject to a unified command on the Western Front, the Allied generalissimo being the redoubtable Marshal Foch. To Rogerson in retrospect there was more than a touch of irony in this new development. He commented :

> It is a sobering reflection that the first act of the unified command was to send battle-shattered British divisions down to rest on the precise sector which barred the road to Paris, and which the enemy had chosen for his next offensive.

It has to be said that for all the talk of laburnum blossom and lilies of the valley the situation was not good from the moment the British arrived. Far from being in a state of congenial relaxation, they found themselves crammed between the front-line trenches and the Aisne, against all the normal rules of military disposition. If attacked, they had nowhere to retire to except a river bank. Even worse, their artillery was similarly placed, in a position of extreme disadvantage. When the commander of this hurriedly flung-together IX Corps, Lieutenant General Sir Archibald Hamilton-Gordon, protested to his French superior, General Duchêne, the latter replied with a comment worthy of Pontius Pilate : " *J'ai dit* " : the French equivalent of Pilate's " What I have written, I have written." He had made his dispositions ; he would not change them.

It has to be admitted that the French believed they had good reasons for not listening to Hamilton-Gordon's pleas, as Rogerson himself conceded, if with a distinct touch of irony, in his first chapter :

> Our gallant allies, however, knew best. They had not had to retreat twice already that year, they allowed us to remember, secretly convinced, no doubt, that it was entirely the fault of the B.E.F. that the Germans had broken through in March and April farther north. No doubt the British knew all about retreats, but they would remain where they were put and obey the orders which the French in their wisdom had issued.

Effectively, by his stubbornness and rigidity, for whatever cause, Duchêne was condemning the British forces suddenly put under his command to the possibility of annihilation. This was one of the main reasons for the writing of this book. Its author wished to show how in an alliance war the decisions of one ally could virtually ordain the humiliation, almost the rout, of another. This should not be allowed to pass unnoticed. A statement should be made. The British on the Aisne in May-June 1918 were, as events turned out, given no chance to defend themselves when the Germans attacked. Instead they were forced to undertake a dispiriting and costly retreat, but a retreat in which, as Rogerson saw it, there was no blame and in which honour was maintained.

Essentially, therefore, this volume is not a ripping account of a death-or-glory battle, or a G. A. Henty romance for real. It is a document of protest, even of some anger, all the more powerful for the idyllic setting in which the events he describes took place and the eloquent, compelling style of his writing.

This was the second of Rogerson's two forceful polemics on the First World War. In 1933 he had written *Twelve Days*, a vivid, unflinching account of a period in the front line in the last fortnight of the Battle of the Somme. His motive in publishing it, however, had not been to regurgitate the so-called horrors of that hard-fought campaign. On the contrary, he had produced it in order to confront those of his generation who, taking a revisionist view of a conflict in which he and countless others had fought with commitment and belief, preferred to focus only on the negative aspects and had no time for the humour, the comradeship and the resolve that had made a tough war bearable. His targets were such writers as the German Erich Maria Remarque, author of *All Quiet on the Western Front*, or Robert Graves, author of *Goodbye to All That*, whom he accused of turning a struggle of high purpose into what he called—in terminology deliberately meant to offend—a " war of the Sewers ".

In other words, Rogerson presented himself, at a time of rising controversy about the purpose and conduct of the First World War, as an advocate for the defence. As in that work, so in this. He was describing what was strictly a defeat—in terms of ground conceded and lives lost, virtually a disgrace—but he was defending it with the full vigour of a committed soldier who was convinced his cause was just. He and all his comrades who had survived that terrible battle of the Aisne could hold their heads high.

In a reversal of the usual roles, he saw the actual ally as almost the enemy, the enemy as a doughty fighter worthy of respect.   Commenting on what he considered a flagrant failure of commitment at an early stage of the retreat, he stated, witheringly : " How those Frenchmen must have 'legged it' ! " As the situation worsened, he began to tap into a feeling that was not entirely new in that war, that something was deeply amiss in this congruence of nations.   In a chapter describing the increasing chaos of the retreat, he wrote : " At this period the conviction was growing among the rank and file that 'we were fighting on the wrong side', a conviction I had heard expressed many times since 1917, but never before with such feeling."

Ironically, it could be said that the German intention, in their strategy for 1918, to separate the British and French was almost being realised, not in terms of prising the two allies apart on the ground, but in a serious—if largely temporary—collapse of mutual trust.

One thing was certain, however.   When Rogerson came to write his book, there would be no question that if he were to invite a soldier from another nation to join him in its production, it would not be a Frenchman, but a German to whom he turned : in fact, the very man to whom had been entrusted the planning of the May 1918 offensive.

The final chapter, entitled " The German Side ", by Major-General A. D. Von Unruh, is integral to the purpose of the book. Chief of Staff of the 4th Reserve Corps, Von Unruh was instructed in April 1918 by his superior in the same trade, the Chief of Staff, German Seventh Army, to undertake a discreet reconnaissance of the Allied positions opposite, to ascertain whether an attack was feasible, and to estimate how many troops would be required. " This was a task surely to delight the heart of any soldier," he wrote in his account, and it was the professional response of an intelligent staff-officer serving his own nation's cause which doubtless appealed to the staff-officer in Sidney Rogerson.

In retrospect there is something deeply moving in this act of friendly collaboration between the Briton and the German, considering that the book was published in 1937, and that two years later Britain and Germany were again at each others' throats. " Operation Blücher " has been well described as an early example of " Blitzkrieg war " ; in 1940 this was the mode of warfare that swept Hitler's *Wehrmacht* across huge swathes of territory in a matter of weeks, condemning the Aisne and all the other sectors of the Western Front, and much of the rest of France, to four years of tragic occupation.

But that was, of course, some way in the future when Rogerson put down his pen. He became the author of several other books, but this was his last about his own military experience. And there can have been only sadness that his friendship with a soldier of distinction who had fought for " our friends the enemy " (his phrase), and whom he clearly greatly admired, must have faded in the dust and destruction of a new and even more terrible conflict.

If there is a further point to be made it is this. One important motive for Rogerson writing his book was to focus public attention on an episode of which little was heard at the time and little has been heard since. The situation pertains to this day. Moreover, if this Second Battle of the Aisne (also known to historians as the Chemin des Dames offensive) has been largely ignored, so has its predecessor, the First Battle of the Aisne, fought in the autumn of 1914 in the wake of the Mons Retreat. Halted by Joffre on the Marne, the Germans reeled back, but not in disarray, instead to make a stand in prepared defence positions on the Aisne heights. There for a period of three to four weeks the opposing armies had their first experience of the kind of warfare for which the war was to become notorious, as enemy confronted enemy in trenches. Suddenly for the British the Germans were no longer blurs of field grey moving at a distance across wide and changing landscapes ; they were dug in the ground perhaps a mere two hundred yards off, so near you could hear them talk, sing, shout orders, yell for stretcher bearers, scream with pain. This was no longer open campaigning ; it was close fighting of a new kind, in essence a twentieth century version of siege warfare. One of the first to see that this was not just a temporary aberration but was likely to become the dominant mode was the then British commander-in-chief, Field Marshal Sir John French, who, in a despatch to King George V on 2nd October, stated : " I think the Battle of the Aisne is very typical of what battles in the future are most likely to resemble. Siege operations will enter largely into the tactical problems—the spade will be as great a necessity as the rifle, and the heaviest calibres and types of artillery will be brought up in support on either side."

There were two to three months more of the war of movement before the long slog of the trenches finally set in, giving the spade and the artillery—the greatest killer in trench conditions—their heyday for most of the next four years. But the fighting on the Aisne had, as it were, put down a marker, sounded a warning, and can, therefore, be seen as crucially affecting the nature of the First World War at its beginning as the 1918 battle affected its outcome.

We are dealing here, therefore, with an area of great historic interest and importance. If Sidney Rogerson's book was written to raise the profile of this hitherto neglected theatre for his generation, then it might be hoped that its republication will, if only in a modest way, perform the same function for people interested in the First World War today.

MALCOLM BROWN
2007

AUTHOR'S INTRODUCTION

IT is related that on the morning of his regimental dinner this year, one young officer was overheard to say to another, " For Heaven's sake stick close to me to-night : I don't want to be put among those old fogies who will insist on discussing the Battle of the Somme ! "

I can sympathise with the speaker, for I was once myself as heartily sick of what in the language of the barrack-room are described as " 'fore you 'listed " tales of the Modder River, Laing's Nek, or Paardeburg. In this sense I feel I should apologise for offering this short narrative of a battle which happened so long ago. It is a somewhat astonishing reflection that the gap between the Great War and to-day is one and a half times as great as that between the South African War and 1914, and very salutary for us veterans to be reminded that our war ended close on twenty years, or nearly a generation, ago.

Still I feel justified in writing for those who survived, especially any who served in those luckless four divisions which, after the bitter ordeals of the first two German onslaughts of 1918, were forced to pass through the fires a third time. I feel justified also because so far this most surprising enemy offensive on the Western Front seems to have escaped attention. As my young subaltern observed, wherever two or three war veterans are gathered together they will discuss, for example, the battles of the Somme, Paschendaele, Loos, or Neuve Chapelle. Such names are common currency among the general reading public. Moreover, they are all actions which were fought in more or less the same circumstances and surroundings : the mud, the barbed wire, the high explosives, the trenches, pill-boxes, and all the stock-in-trade of the scene-painter of the World War. The battle of the Aisne was something different, just as it was more immediately successful from the enemy's point of view and more disastrous from the point of view of the French or British. At no other time was a British army corps so nearly annihilated as was the IXth Corps between the Aisne and Marne in May 1918. Fighting under French command, inadequately supported by artillery and practically without help from the air, the four tired divisions were forced to fight and run, fight and walk, twenty-seven miles in four days across wooded downlands and three fair rivers, in brilliant summer weather and subsisting on a mixture of hard emergency rations and the good wine of Champagne. It was an astonishing battle in a novel setting, and it contained many notable feats of arms. It should therefore be better known.

The outline of my narrative was jotted down very soon after the Armistice, when my experiences were still fresh in mind, so that I can claim that it records the events and reproduces the atmosphere of those days as nearly as may be. Its disadvantage is that, as I was a subordinate infantry officer, I can only describe the battle as it unrolled around me on one short sector of the widely stretched arc. It is not therefore for me to speak of the strategy behind the action, or to show how the plan was carried into effect.   Fortunately, through the agency of friends in Germany, General Von Unruh has been persuaded to deal with this aspect, than whom no fitter person could have been found, for to Von Unruh more than to any other man must be given the credit for this last brilliant effort of German arms. It was he, as chief of staff of the Army Corps of General von Conta, who planned the assault against the strongest point of the Allied line, the great natural bastion of the Chemin des Dames and the Californie Plateau, known to the Germans as the Winterberg; and it was his corps which not only burst a way through our lines for its neighbours on both flanks to enlarge, but drove determinedly on to reach the Marne.

Though the original front of Von Unruh's assault brushed closely past the left of our Brigade, the south-westerly direction of the German advance after the second day, May 28, carried it away from the sector we strove to defend.   Yet the picture he paints with such economy covers the whole canvas, opposing the scene viewed through the eyes of the attacking General Staff to that seen by the defending infantry soldier.   More-over, it records with characteristic reserve the wave of high hopes raised by the initial break-through and the bitter disappointment when this was shattered five days later.   For if for us the battle was the last of the ebb, for the Germans it was the top of the flow, a spring tide the tactical success of which was the measure of its strategic failure.   Shortage of men, as General Von Unruh explains, had necessitated a restricted frontage of attack which, though adequate for Ludendorff's modest original objectives, was quite unsound as the chord of an offensive in depth.   The result was a long, narrow salient, and though from its apex the eager

THE LAST
OF THE EBB

THE SHRUBBERY

I

THE SHRUBBERY

On May 5, 1918, the battle-weary units of the 8th Division detrained at Fère-en-Tardenois, and, for the second time during the war, British troops found themselves in the country between the Aisne and the Marne.

The Division had been terribly shattered in both German offensives on the Somme in March, and at Villers Bretonneux in April, and sorely needed rest and respite. But rest behind the line was impossible owing to the shortage of men, and on the British front there were no longer quiet sectors where tired divisions could, while holding the line, regain their energy and assimilate their heavy reinforcements. Such homes of rest were only to be found on the front held by the French armies, and so it came about that at the beginning of May the IXth Corps was formed of the 8th, 21st, 25th, and 50th Divisions and, under the recently effected unity in the Allied High Command, was transferred to the 6th French Army taking over a section about fifteen miles in length between Rheims and the Chemin des Dames.

To battered, battle-weary troops, whose only knowledge of France was based upon their experience of the Northern front, the Champagne country in the full glory of spring was a revelation. Gone

was the depressing monotony of Flanders, drab
and weeping, with its muds, its mists, its pollards,
and its pavé ; gone the battle-wrecked landscapes
of Picardy and the Somme, with their shattered
villages and blasted woods. Here all was peace.
The countryside basked contentedly in the blazing
sunshine. Trim villages nestled in quiet hollows
beside lazy streams, and tired eyes were refreshed
by the sight of rolling hills, clad with great woods
golden with laburnum blossom ; by the soft
greenery of lush meadowland, shrubby vineyards
and fields of growing corn. Right up to within
two miles of the line civilians were living, going
about their business of husbandry with characteristic
unconcern.

Nor was the illusion of rustic tranquillity dispelled by the trench area itself, although this had
been the scene of the bloody and disastrous French
offensive of 1917. The ground was everywhere
pitted with shell-holes, honeycombed with dug-outs,
and littered with tangles of barbed wire. Here
were concrete " pill-boxes," super " pill-boxes,"
like square forts and all pockmarked by gun-fire.
There, in a line, the charred remains of seven or
eight tanks—a grim memento of the disastrous
first use of these weapons by the French. But
whereas only a year before it had been an area of
death and destruction, in May 1918 Nature had
reasserted herself and cloaked the grosser evidences
of battle with a mantle of green. Only the actual
front-line trenches, dug in the chalk, seared the
landscape with white scars. The woods had been
blasted by the shell-fire of the previous year, but
now each shattered tree stump had covered its

wounds with a wealth of close foliage. In the shell-holes grass had grown and water-plants. Near the gun emplacements in the reserve line grew lilies-of-the-valley, forget-me-nots, larkspur, and honey-suckle. The whole battle area had become a shrubbery fashioned by artillery. Among the reeds of the Aisne River I hunted swallow-tail butterflies and rare Camberwell Beauties, and even found a whitethroat's nest with eggs.

In places coils of rusty wire showed redly through the grass, and the derelict tanks and shattered pill-boxes still resisted all Nature's attempts to conceal the handiwork of war. Occasionally, too, a shell would break the summer silence and wake echoes in the sleeping hills. But even the shells seemed tired, arriving in a leisurely sort of way and exploding apologetically, without injury to any one. These were small blemishes. They served, if anything, to increase rather than diminish the general impression that in such a setting hostilities were impossible—appearing rather as relics from some hideous past, instead of as the coffin at the feast.

So forceful was the illusion that even the French Command appeared to have been lulled into a sense of security, and this in spite of the fact that it was admitted that the enemy had had an attack " mounted " on this front for a considerable time. Indeed, the French had already made extensive counter-preparations and had heavily fortified the Roucy heights, a range of steep, heavily wooded hills marking the southern slopes of the Aisne valley.

The actual sector taken over by the IXth British Corps lay between Bermicourt and Bouconville, north-west of Rheims, the 50th Division holding the left, the 8th the centre, and the 21st the right. The 25th Division arrived a few days later and was placed in reserve. The 8th Division's sector formed a pronounced salient pushed out into the German lines, and the Division was disposed with all three brigades in line, each on a one-battalion front. My own Brigade, the 23rd, took the left flank and were ordered to relieve the 371st French territorial regiment, commanded by a fat dug-out major, whose headquarters were at Bois des Buttes, close by the picturesquely named one-time village of Ville-au-Bois.

Under our Brigadier, W. G. St. G. Grogan, of the Worcester Regiment, 23rd Brigade Head-quarters were a very happy and youthful family, consisting of Howard Millis of the Sherwood Foresters, Brigade-major ; P. A. Ledward, Hamp-shire Regiment, Staff-captain ; Kenneth Thompson, West Yorkshires, Intelligence ; Parsloe, Devons, Transport Officer ; Prance, South Wales Borderers, the Signal Officer, and the baby of the mess; and myself. My job was indeterminate, a sort of " dogsbody " to take the place of any one who went on leave or to do any work not specifically covered by the others. The day before the relief we all, except Parsloe, accompanied the Brigadier on the customary visit to the French to meet our opposite numbers and make arrangements for taking over our respective duties. It was a diverting experience. The regiment had been holding the sector for two months and had made themselves very comfortable. It was not their policy to disturb the enemy. He, in turn, we gathered, did not disturb them. Still we were surprised and a little

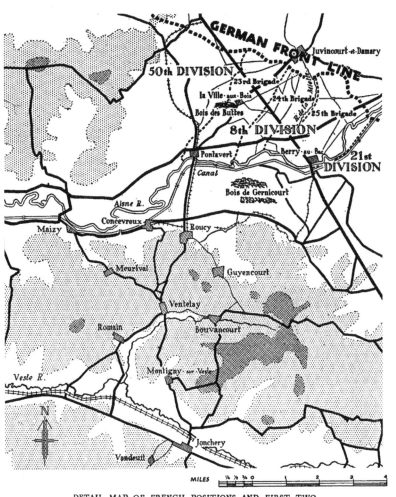

DETAIL MAP OF FRENCH POSITIONS AND FIRST TWO
DAYS FIGHTING OF 8TH DIVISION.

shocked to find that the French C.O., had never
been up to the front line : " The Intelligence Officer
is often there," it was explained ; " he is very
brave." Moreover, instead of our being expected
to spend the time over the sternly practical details
of a trench-relief, the programme centred in a
ceremonial repast. At the height of the May noon
we sat down with our French friends in a dug-out,
the small door of which served to keep out the
daylight but not the heat, and faced the succession
of dishes and wines that are considered proper in
France on occasions of solemnity or rejoicing.
Afterwards, when we were all very hot and very
conscious of what we had eaten, the Major delivered
an oration, declaring how honoured he was to hand
over his trust to his English allies. The trouble
was that such a speech compelled an answer and
the Brigadier was not only no speaker, but knew
little French. Still, if his delivery was halting and
his accent atrocious, the sentiments he expressed
were suitably heroic. " We would defend to the
last man the ground sanctified by so much French
blood," and " The enemy would only pass over
our bodies." It was all rather embarrassing and
not a little ludicrous at the time, and in the days to
come I was to wonder more than once how much
of it had been remembered.

We left with the conviction that the relief would
be, in the vernacular of the period, " a proper
bloody box-up." We had neither succeeded in
reconnoitring for ourselves the various communication trenches nor in pinning the French down to
detail on any point. The feeling was increased
when we got copies of the French relief orders,

however much these stirred us to mirth. They consisted of about four sentences—little more than statements of fact—and ended with the words, " Pas de manœuvres de lampes électriques ; en cas de bombardement on se couche ! " Never did such simple instructions serve to cover such a multitude of contingencies !

Our fears proved groundless, and the change-over of French and English was effected with hardly a hitch, much assisted by the complete inaction of the enemy. It may also have been helped by the absence of the French commanding officer. He had been recognised as a fussy old gentleman, and I was entrusted with the task of keeping him out of the way until the relief was complete, a task I accomplished with the aid of the mess port and whisky. After sampling " le porto," he admitted his preference for whisky, which he drank neat. The night being hot it was not surprising that his tongue was loosened, and he was soon regaling me with a recital of his war experiences. Among the many decorations on his jacket—they were dotted without any attempt at order up and down his ample frame from his left breast to his navel— was the familiar red and blue of our Distinguished Conduct Medal. " Figurez-vous, mon vieux," he said, tapping this with a pudgy forefinger. " Your Prince of Connaught signalled me out as the bravest man in three corps d'armée to present me with this." Meanwhile the business of handing-over proceeded smoothly.

Toward the early hours the relief was announced as complete, the French said their adieux and moved out, leaving us in possession. Besides being a

salient—and Ypres had taught us the discomforts
of such !—the trench system that we held was only
a matter of one and a half miles in front of the
Aisne River, with which ran parallel at a distance
of about one hundred yards the Aisne Canal. These
two waterways in turn were almost parallel with the
line on our immediate front, and a third, the Miette,
flowed between marshy banks to join the Aisne
between the sectors held by our right and centre
brigades (25th and 24th) which were thus cut off
from one another. According to the dispositions
which, in accordance with French orders, we had
taken up, the battle-stations of all troops were on
the German side of the Aisne, and our artillery
were in emplacements used by the French for
months, and, consequently, it was safe to argue,
well known to the enemy. 8th Divisional Headquarters were in Roucy village, about four miles
in rear, where the staff was billeted in the château
perched upon a hillside in full view of the German
trenches.

These were tactical mistakes of the first order,
and obvious to the youngest subaltern, but at the
time we pooh-poohed the likelihood of any activity
which might necessitate battle-stations being taken
up.

What we mercifully did not know was the grave
anxiety that these dispositions and the French
orders concerning them was causing at the headquarters of the three divisions in the British corps.
Not only was the bulk of our forces, infantry and
artillery, to be posted on the German side of the
Aisne, but this narrow strip of ground, part of which
was also an all-too-vulnerable salient, was to be

held at all costs. It was to form the battle zone, and any reserves which might be available were to be thrown in to retake any part of it which might be lost to the enemy. Explicit orders from the French Command were that not a yard of ground was to be given up. It is worth laying stress on the imbecility of such orders if only for the benefit of those who are still prone to believe that British staff work was so much below the level of that of the other combatants, allied or hostile. They were the subject of a vigorous protest by Sir Alexander Hamilton Gordon, G.O.C. IXth Corps, who pointed out the suicidal folly of stationing the troops in well-marked defences in front of the natural obstacles of the Aisne and its canal, suggesting that these would be better utilised as additional defences to the main battle line.

Our gallant allies, however, knew best. They had not had to retreat twice already that year, they allowed us to remember, secretly convinced, no doubt, that it was entirely the fault of the B.E.F. that the Germans had broken through in March and April farther north. No doubt the British knew all about retreats, but they would remain where they were put and obey the orders which the French in their wisdom had issued.

Half-left from us, and on the farther flank of the 50th Division, ran the hog's-back of the Chemin des Dames, a mountain range in miniature, held by the 22nd French Division. Also on our left, in the 50th Divisional area, was the famous Californie Plateau or Winterberg as the Germans called it, with its blasted crest gleaming dazzling white in the sun. On our own divisional front the ground was uniformly flat, only broken by the Bois des Buttes, which rose like a giant mole-hill from the plain, a perfect reference mark for the German gunner ; and on our right was the low valley of the Aisne.

Except for this topographical prominence, the Bois des Buttes was an ideal headquarters. Around its base deep shafts led down to a regular underground barracks, thirty feet below ground level, excavated originally by the enemy and improved by the French. Apart from the burrows actually running under the hillock itself and occupied by the personnel of Brigade Headquarters, were three other sets of tunnels, all lighted by electricity and big enough if necessary to hide three battalions, in addition to the heterogeneous collection of British artillery observers and French electrical mechanics, anti-tank gunners, and heavy-machine gunners already located in them. Indeed, an entire German regiment had, we were told, been found in them when taken a year previously. They had since been much enlarged and improved, and there were two entrances into which ran miniature railways and big enough to allow the passage of a 3-ton lorry.

As living quarters at this time of the year they were suffocatingly hot, but into the sides of the Bois des Buttes roomier shelters had been built enjoying both light and air. Our mess, offices, and sleeping quarters were in these ground-floor dwellings, out of which opened the stairs to the underground bolt-holes. The General's bedroom was a particularly imposing apartment, containing a large four-poster bed, a legacy reluctantly left behind by the French major.

At the other side of the hill in similar habitations and connected by the underground passages, were the headquarters of the artillery brigade which was covering our front. This was the 45th Brigade R.F.A., now described in conformity with French practice as " La Groupe Ballard " after their C.O., Colonel Ballard. It was at once a tactical and a social convenience to have the gunners so close—not only were we in close touch with artillery support, but we never lacked a fourth at bridge at night !

From the dug-outs a perpendicular chimney had been pierced through the centre of the hill, opening at the summit in a heavily protected concrete look-out post. On a forward spur, facing the line, was the regular day observation post.

The Bois des Buttes was in short a defensive position of great potential strength. The trouble was that its vast and ramified systems of tunnels was never half-explored nor a quarter used.

Similarly with the trenches. In every direction ran trenches, some relics of German occupation, some dug by the French and never used, some filled with wire, some with grass and brambles. I was told off to explore them, and for ten days struggled to follow them on the ground and on the maps handed over by the French, but without much success. Dignified by high-sounding names —" première parallèle de doublement," " deuxième ligne de réduits," "ligne de surveillance "—most of them were disused and overgrown. My efforts were joined by those of others at Headquarters and in the regiments, but it was humanly impossible in the time at our disposal to reconnoitre the trench

area properly, much less to organise it into an
adequate scheme of defence.   Moreover, we were
strung out on such a wide front that the garrison
of even the front line was pitifully thin and there
were no men available to man the strong points or
switch lines in rear.   We had therefore meta-
phorically to shrug our shoulders and rely on the
parting assurance of the French, " The line is very
strong : there is much wire."   The last part of this
remark was certainly true.   There were such
quantities that it was difficult to move freely any-
where in the forward area except along one of the
regular communication trenches.

I did trace the main communication trench which
ran from Bois des Buttes to Pontavert village, but
I think I was the only man who ever did so, as it
was quite safe—and of course much less trouble—
to use the road.   No one succeeded in reconnoitring the other bridges across the river.   There
must have been over twenty of these all told on the
divisional front, but most of them were in the areas
of the 24th and 25th Brigades.   The only one we
actually knew in our own area was that at Pontavert,
though we took it for granted there was one which
led to the Bois de Gernicourt, a strong point south
of the river on which it was ordered that we should
fall back if compelled to do so.

But none of these things seriously worried us.
We had come down to the French front for a rest-
cure.   We expected neither to attack nor to be
attacked.   Yet it was partly due to this combina-
tion of circumstances that the enemy was able so
successfully to make his break-through.

Our first week in the line passed peacefully

enough. At Brigade Headquarters we all found plenty of work to do in reorganising the area as far as possible on English lines.

Our quarters were luxurious indeed compared with anything to which we had hitherto been accustomed. Why, they were actually lit by electricity, though this was not an unmixed blessing. It was supplied by an engine in charge of a French mechanic who lived in some corner of the catacombs below us. This very grimy gentleman we soon suspected of practising a species of blackmail, as he quickly developed a taste for English bread and ration jam (incidentally we never solved the mystery of how these scattered French details got their rations). If no jam was forthcoming, he would shortly appear and announce, " Plus d'essence," and we had no light ! There was then the complication that as the British Army did not provide for any issue of petrol for lighting the trench homes of the infantry, we had to beg a gallon or so at a time as a favour from the C.R.E., and so were frequently without light.

Another minor affliction was a surprise visit paid us by the French Army Commander, meet to be recorded if only because it was the occasion of probably the worst piece of pidgin-French ever publicly uttered. Uncertain how far it was safe to bring his car, the great man had stopped it some distance in rear of Bois des Buttes and walked, leaving instructions, he informed us, for it to follow him slowly. It was important that it should not come abreast of the hillock for it would then be in full view from the German line and likely to draw fire. One senior British officer, whose identity it is only fair to conceal, hastily informed the General : " Je vais stationner un sentinel pour bloquer l'auto ! " To stop M. le Général's car coming too far, I had to explain in French. Incidentally none of the French spoke English and few indeed understood any, with the result that I was in constant demand as an interpreter, whether to deal with mechanics or visiting brass-hats. During the three years I was in France I reached the conclusion that there were many more Englishmen who spoke and understood French than *vice versa*, in spite of all that my schoolmaster had told me about the English being the worst linguists in Europe. The linguistic inferiority of the English soon appeared to me as much of a myth as the reputed chic and attractiveness of the Frenchwomen. Both, I reflected, might at one time have been true, but had ceased to be axiomatic by 1914.

Whenever we were off duty we seized the opportunity of calling on old friends in the regiments or the batteries whom we had had no chance of seeing since the war of movement had begun two months before. Close to us were the 2nd West Yorkshires, the support battalion, who inhabited the garden suburb around the Bois des Buttes, where they could pick lilies-of-the-valley at their dug-out doors. Farther back across the Aisne the 2nd Middlesex were in billets as reserve battalion and thoroughly enjoyed themselves. They held a regimental sports day, when Lieut.-Colonel C. C. Page found scope for his humour in some novel competitions. One deserving of special mention was for sanitary men who were required to build a latrine out of " unpromising material "—" marks to be awarded for

comfort, decency, and speed of construction ! "
In the front line the 2nd Devons found life uneventful though they complained of the heat and
an inadequate water supply. The heat was intense,
and the chalk trenches seemed to convert themselves
into ovens of glaring whiteness.

The communication trenches were particularly
hot as they were much deeper than those made by
the British, chiefly, I imagine, on account of the
use made by the French of small donkeys for carrying rations up to the line. The processions of ten
or fifteen little " burros " piled heavens high with
sacks and boxes, stepping stiffly up a trench with
the donkey-herd behind them making uncouth
noises of encouragement or reproof, never failed
to amuse our men. Indeed we were all both amused
and interested. The whole scene was so novel,
and the atmosphere of tranquillity so refreshing
after the months of drab monotony and battle-
racket that we could not well be otherwise.

THE AISNE

II

THE AISNE

AFTER eight days the first inter-brigade relief took place, the West Yorkshires moving into the front line and the Middlesex up into support. The Devons retired to Roucy for a rest and clean-up.

It was about this time that the serpent entered our Eden. An uneasy feeling began to spread among us that all was not well. Bear in mind that there was a core of officers and men who had been through both the great German offensives and whose suspicions were readily aroused as much because they were determined if possible not to be trapped again, as because their nerves were excusably enough on edge. Unlike the French whose policy was never to disturb a wasps' nest unless and until you meant to take it, we were accustomed to a front where continuous harassing of the Germans was the rule. A quiet enemy was an enemy to be suspected if not feared. And there was no doubt about it—the enemy was much too quiet.

So we looked for confirmation of our fears and soon found it. Thompson's intelligence men noted that the German balloons, especially one behind Juvincourt, were being pulled down and run up again and moved about with great frequency. There was more railway movement and the German gunners seemed to wake to life. True, there was no shelling such as we had become inured to farther north, but there was an increase in the steady, methodical " crumping " of battery positions, one shell at a time. This was significant in that the suspicious-minded could only put it down to ranging or the calibration of new guns. Colour was lent to this view by the fact that once on the target the shelling ceased.

8th Division accordingly decided that some definite information must be obtained. " Patrolling must be pressed with energy and identification secured." This identification was found to be difficult to get. The enemy were very much alert and had, moreover, withdrawn from their first two lines of trenches, which they had wired up. This in itself was disquieting.

At last something happened. A West Yorkshire patrol of one officer and three men succeeded in getting through the German wire and collided with an enemy patrol of some twenty men. Bombs were thrown and one of our men killed. Taking the dead man with them, the patrol drew off. Unluckily they were no sooner in No-Man's-Land again than they met a second German patrol. A further exchange of bombs resulted in a German being killed, but the West Yorkshires had another man wounded, and were forced to retire, abandoning the dead man—a regrettable occurrence, as it told the enemy definitely that British troops were in line before him. On his return the officer in charge of the patrol handed in a shoulder strap which he had found near the German wire, and which bore the number of an enemy regiment not previously known to be on the Aisne front. Great excitement prevailed at Divisional Headquarters on this discovery, and the wires to all parts of the allied front were kept busy trying to get corroboration.

Eventually the reply came that the German regiment in question had been definitely located at another part of the line, being one with which we had been engaged on the Somme a month before. Still, the mystery remained until one of the West Yorkshire intelligence section who had been on the patrol confessed that he had lost a shoulder strap taken from a German at Villers Bretonneux. By which it is seen that whole armies can be much put about by such a casual thing as a private soldier dropping an apparently harmless souvenir !

No identification having been secured, the West Yorkshires again sent out a patrol, which went at once to the body of the German killed the night previously, only to discover that the enemy had been thorough. Every distinguishing mark had been stripped from the man's uniform, every incriminating document apparently taken from his pockets. It was to the lasting credit of the officer leading the patrol that he refused to admit himself beaten. With great care he searched the corpse and was rewarded by finding in a hip-pocket a scrap of envelope bearing the address and unit of the dead man.

The information was reassuring. The regiment opposite us was one which had been long in line. They were merely holding troops. They would not attack. We breathed again.

Our respite was short-lived, and from that moment events moved rapidly.

One morning three pathetic figures stumbled

into the front line, French soldiers escaped from captivity. They were eagerly cross-examined. Had they noticed unusual activity behind the enemy lines ? Yes, the prisoners' camps were being emptied, great masses of troops were arriving, everywhere was bustle and movement. In the German support trenches were guns dug in up to the muzzle.

A day later the Intelligence Officer of the 24th Brigade reported the presence of a number of black boards between the German trenches. These could only be the direction boards known to be used for the guidance of tanks or heavy transport.

Then from the French on the left came the final blow. News that a great enemy attack was impending was elicited from three members of a German patrol captured on the Chemin des Dames. On further special examination, the prisoners confessed that this would open at midnight, May 26–27, by German time.

The first news of this reached us about 3.45 p.m. on May 26. In a shallow trench outside the mess dug-out, Millis and I were stretching ourselves in the sun. A signaller came up and handed Millis the little pink telephone slip. He read it and without a word passed it to me. " The enemy will attack on a wide front at 01.00 hours to-morrow, 27th inst. : A.A.A."—then followed orders for taking up battle stations.

For a second we looked at each other in silence. In a flash the whole world had changed. The landscape around us smiled no longer. It was all a grinning reality, a mockery designed to raise our hopes so that they could be shattered the more pitilessly. The sun still blazed down but it had lost its heat. Millis said something like " Oh, well, it can't be helped. We're for it again," and went off to break the news to the General.

So the blow had fallen. For the third time we were to bear the brunt of an enemy offensive. Surely we who had suffered so much already might have been spared this! It was too much to hope that those of us who had come through so far would again escape. The mercy was that we had little time to indulge in self-pity. Everything was haste and energy. Moments were of importance. Much had to be done before zero hour; the biggest single item being to reconnoitre dug-out accommodation for the 2nd Devons, who would form the garrison of the reserve or battle line which ran on a level with the Bois des Buttes. This task was left to Ledward and me and a hot and tiring one it was, involving much climbing of crazy stairs and hurrying, bent double, along low corridors. We were staggered at the size and extent of this underground village, and more than once lost our way. The Devons had never seen the position or been in the tunnels, and as they would only arrive after dark we dared not imagine how they were likely to fare.

About 6.30 p.m. there arrived from French Army Headquarters a signal officer to inspect communications in the Brigade area. He was informed that our signal officer, Prance, was busy up the line supervising arrangements for the morrow's attack. This was apparently the first intimation that the Frenchman had had of the impending offensive, but the news merely caused a smile. What, the enemy attack? Nonsense, they had been *going* to attack for four months on this front, but of course every one knew they never would. " Ils sont plus sages que ça. On ne passerait jamais ici." It is more than probable that he left Bois des Buttes convinced that the English were very " windy."

His departure coincided with the arrival of the officer in charge of the French " mitrailleuses de position," heavy Etienne machine-guns which had been left as an additional garrison to the line. None of us knew their locations, but the grey-haired old French captain called to place himself under British command and assure the British general of his unswerving obedience—a pleasant interlude, reminiscent of more chivalrous days, at a time when chivalry was at a discount.

It was a splendid evening, and as the sun waned and we stood on our hillock waiting for dinner we looked down on the scene around us, across the green shrubbery where the smoke from the Middle-sex cook-houses rose in thin blue pillars through the still air, and over to the trees and reeds that marked the course of the Aisne River. It was all so peaceful and so vibrant with life, yet by to-morrow's light what would have happened? High overhead, mere black spots in the soft amber haze were two German planes quartering the ground like hovering kestrels and noting the every movement of the tiny mice below. Not a gun fired at them, nor friendly aeroplane went to drive them off, for the French, it seemed, had neither " Archies " nor aircraft available. For the first time in the war I had the feeling that there was no one behind us, no help which could be relied upon in case of need to stem a breach or retake a vital point.

Dinner was not an enjoyable meal, and as soon as it was over the more prudent, or the more pessimistic, as it then seemed, set to work to pack up everything not absolutely necessary. I was one who had a horror of being caught short of minor necessities, so carefully crammed into a pack a spare pair of boots and socks, a shirt, vest, tin of cigarettes, matches, and a bottle of whisky. I got definite satisfaction out of this, as I felt that somehow it was the only preparation it lay in my power to make against any eventuality the next morning might bring, and it was not till months later that I realised how futile it must have appeared in the eyes of Heaven—as well might I have buttoned my overcoat to ward off the lightning ! Most of the others took a more sanguine or more fatalistic view and did not bother. This cost General Grogan a beautiful brand-new uniform and many items of out-of-the-trenches apparel that he had had sent up to the Bois des Buttes preparatory to going on short leave to Paris !

A message came in about 9 o'clock giving the names of a number of men who had been sent up that night to rejoin their units from hospital, leave, or other duties. Among these was my servant, Private Briggs,[1] posted back to the West Yorkshires from hospital. He had been with me since October 1916, but had gone sick early in March, and I had temporarily taken on the venerable Mr. Parkin, my one-time cook, in his place. It would happen, I thought, that Briggs should have been sent to the

[1] See " Twelve Days."

regiment direct on the eve of a battle, when I had no chance of applying for him back again ! It was fifteen years before I was to see him again.

Meanwhile it was growing dark. The transport arrived early, bringing rations and ammunition and taking away any surplus kit that was ready to be moved, but they did not tarry long. The Devons began moving into their tunnels. With the coming of night, an uncanny silence settled over the country-side, a silence such as can only prevail in crowded places. About nine o'clock " harassing " fire was opened on enemy communications and assembly points. All along our line the batteries gave tongue, the sharp bang of eighteen-pounders mingling with the hoarse reports of the field howitzers. Behind the river the few old French " heavies," regular museum pieces, coughed asthmatically now and again, while the intermittent dry rattle of machine-guns came as a staccato punctuation. Still, the feeling of silence persisted. Not a gun was fired by the enemy, and his quietness dispelled any last lingering hopes we might have cherished. How that evening dragged ! The minutes crept slowly towards zero hour. I had gone into the mess to inquire from Johns, our imperturbable mess-corporal, whether he was all packed-up ready to move if necessary. I took a whisky-and-soda and was standing talking to him when suddenly whizz—plop ! whizz—plop ! Two German gas shells burst close at hand, punctual heralds of the storm. Within a second a thousand guns roared out their iron hurricane. The night was rent with sheets of flame. The earth shuddered under the avalanche of missiles : leapt skywards in dust and tumult.

Ever above the din screamed the fierce crescendo of approaching shells, ear-splitting crashes as they burst : all the time the dull thud, thud, thud of detonations—drumfire . . . Inferno raged and whirled round the Bois des Buttes. The dug-outs rocked, filled with the acrid fumes of cordite, the sickly-sweet tang of gas. Timbers started. Earth showered from the roof. Men rushed for shelter, seizing kits, weapons, gas-masks, message-pads as they dived to safety. It was a descent into hell. Crowded with jostling, sweating humanity, the deep dug-outs reeked, and to make matters worse, we had no sooner got below than gas began to filter down. Gas-masks were hurriedly donned and anti-gas precautions taken—the entrances closed by saturated blankets, braziers lighted on the stairs. If gas could not enter, neither could air—though the fact was that in small quantities both did. Mercifully that night was short in time however long it seemed, otherwise we could not have endured, crammed as we were into stinking, overcrowded holes, forty feet below ground, all the entrances sealed up and charcoal braziers burning, heaving to get a breath of oxygen through the gas-mask with its clip on nostrils and its gag between teeth. At first my heart thumped and my head swam distressingly, but I found if I kept still I could just bear it.

Down below the clamour of the barrage was muted, but even so far underground the walls shivered every few minutes as a heavy shell burst directly overhead. The Brigadier, Millis, Ledward, Prance and I were together, Thompson having already gone to his observation post. Prance's signallers at once made contact with the battalions

and the flank brigades—149th on the left and 24th
on the right—both by 'phone and wire.   The
other Brigade Headquarters were undergoing
experiences like our own, but the West Yorkshires
reported cheerily, " We're all right. You're getting
the worst of it. It's going over us "—then the
line went dead, and we heard no more from the
front line battalion. The Middlesex, close to us,
were being terribly pounded, though they were
reasonably safe so long as they kept below ground.
Up to then the gunners had come off worst. The
first surge of the barrage had overwhelmed them,
the 24th Brigade's (Ballard) emplacements having
been so accurately registered that after half an hour
they had only one gun left in action.

These and other messages from 8th Division
reached us as we sat huddled up on the frame-
beds round the dug-out walls. Prance had soon
grown restless and, clapping on his helmet, had
gone out to be with his men who were working
to keep the wires intact. He would not take an
orderly, saying he felt happier without one—a
point of view I could not understand.   The
Brigadier was also, very naturally, restless. He too
would have preferred to be out and alone in danger,
rather than cooped up, inactive but in safety, but
his place was for the moment at the end of the
telephone. Millis was calmness itself, and I was
too nearly stifled and too busy to feel more than
usually fearful. I had been given the job of keeping
a diary of the action, to include every outgoing and
incoming message. This had been declared necessary because the absence of such records in the two
earlier offensives had made it impossible to trace

the sequence of events or even to tell what had happened. So I wrote messages at Millis's dictation, and passed them to Signals, keeping a copy for myself. Similarly I collected every incoming message, whether verbal or Morse.

Dawn began to break outside, but no news reached us that the enemy had yet attacked. Thompson reported that a very heavy ground mist, joined with the smoke and dust of the bombardment, made observation impossible over a few yards. The thump !—thud !—thump !—thud ! overhead told us the barrage continued. Perhaps the Germans were not going to attack on our front after all ! Vain hope ! Not five minutes after his first statement Thompson sent the amazing message : " Can see enemy balloons rising from our front line ! " Hot upon this came another from the 24th Brigade on our right : " Enemy advancing up Miette stream. Close to Brigade Headquarters. Cannot hold out without reinforcements." Such news was startling enough, but worse was yet to come, and shortly afterwards—at about 5.30 a.m.—the left flank brigade, 149th, reported, " Enemy has broken our battle-line and is advancing on Ville au Bois."

Before a word had come that our front had been assaulted, the enemy had turned both flanks and was closing on the Bois des Buttes. For the second time, our world had altered in a flash. Our position was no longer a stronghold but a death-trap. There was nothing left but to obey orders and fall back across the Aisne—a decision no sooner taken than acted upon. Men struggled into their battle equipment as they clambered up the steep stairs, abandoning everything except the office con-

fidential dispatch-box.   I hitched my precious
pack on my shoulders.   In it was now the diary and
wad of messages.

What a scene met us as we floundered into the
light of the young day !   Everywhere was ruin,
desolation thinly veiled by mist and smoke.   The
barrage had begun to lift a little but was still very
heavy, and the line of the Aisne spouted black
where big shells were bursting.   The party stood
about uncertain which way to take.   " Rogerson,"
the Brigadier yelled above the racket, "you know
the way by the trench, don't you ?   Well, lead
on ! "

Wanting no second bidding, I put my head
down—the instinctive action of a man fronting a
storm—and dashed off into the whirling cordite
dust which filled the trench.   The goggles of my
gas-mask fogged before I had run twenty yards.
I collided violently with the trench wall, turned to
see how the others were following—and found I
was alone !   Then did Terror, which had been
dogging my thoughts since the afternoon before,
take hold of me.   At any second one of those
screaming missiles might rend me, stretch me
bleeding but conscious on the battered earth,
where I should lie till Death or a not-too-kindly
enemy should find me.   My fear in that moment
was not of death but of disablement.   I was not
like young Prance.   To share danger with others
was bearable, to be alone was terrifying.   Back I
turned to our abandoned dug-outs, where, merciful
relief, I stumbled into two gunner officers starting
out according to orders to reach the Bois de Gernicourt.   None of us knew the way, so made a blind

point across country towards the Aisne. What a
flight that was—across shell-holes, through barbed-
wire, brambles, and the twisted and shattered
remains of shelters and gun-pits ; stumbling,
falling, sweating, the steel helmet bobbing on my
head, the heavy pack between my shoulders ;
breathless, gasping wide-open-mouthed into the
gas-mask whose clip so firmly closed my nostrils.
How we got there I shall never know, but somehow
there stretched before us the reeds and willows of
the river, along which a steady barrage of large-
calibre shells was falling, sending up tall geysers
of black mud. Frantically we searched upstream
and down for a bridge, but there was no sign.
From somewhere behind us came the slow rattle of
a German machine-gun. That settled it, and
throwing off helmets, gas-masks, and jackets, the
others plunged into the current and were soon
across, although the elder of them, I learned afterwards, lost his false teeth in the effort ! I followed,
and on the sudden realised that all the time I had
been clutching in my right hand the signal-book
which held copies of the last messages we had
sent out. Holding this out of the water, I tried to
swim with my left arm alone, but in my heavily
loaded state—for I still clung to gas-mask, helmet,
and pack—this was impossible. I went under.
My gas-mask filled. Water went up my nose
and down my throat, choking me. Struggling back
to the bank, I tore off the mask and tried again, and
again sank. This time it was my pack, with its
personal comforts and official records that had to
go, but the sacrifice was without avail. I was too
exhausted ever to have got across. Damn the

Bois de Gernicourt!   Instead, alone again, I ploughed along through nettles, rushes, docks, and shell-bursts towards the bridge I knew to be at Pontavert. To my amazement I found it was just round a bend in the river, not two hundred yards away !

What had happened to the Brigadier and the rest of Headquarters ?   Apparently he had no sooner told me to lead the way by trench than some one pointed out to him that although the road to Pontavert was receiving particular attention from the enemy gunners, it was the quickest and most direct route to a river-crossing.   To attempt to lead a party cross-country in search of the Bois de Gernicourt was held to be out of the question. Accordingly, the main body moved off, with the Brigadier leading and two of the clerks bearing the tin dispatch-box.   Although flying splinters of shell rang on steel helmets and clipped great pieces from the road, the little gas-goggled procession wound its way to Pontavert untouched.   Others were less fortunate.   Thompson, for example, told us later in the day that we only just got out of the Bois des Buttes in the nick of time, as German infantry closed on the hillock in strength not five minutes later.   From his observation post he had seen vast numbers of the enemy advancing almost unopposed and therefore retired with his six observers, "four of whom were either killed or wounded before we crossed the Aisne."

All this I was to learn afterwards, and at the time all I knew was that as I, a filthy, dripping, dishevelled figure, staggered on to the bridge at Pontavert, I was surprised to find the Brigadier standing there, crook-handled stick in hand, quietly directing the walking-wounded and collecting the few stragglers who were beginning to trickle back in a thin stream. Beside him was an overturned G.S. wagon and the bodies of its horses, a pair of chestnuts, which even in that instant I recognised as the pride of my regiment's transport. Farther on was an 8th Divisional Staff-car in which was Bourdillon, the D.A.D.M.S. I was without arms, without gas-mask, I had lost the diary I had kept, and my sodden clothes clung on me like poultices. With General Grogan's permission, I got a lift in Bourdillon's car back to Roucy, and within ten minutes was sitting in the relative security of a house behind the firing line. Here D.A.D.O.S. took compassion on me, and although almost all his kit and stores were packed up ready to leave, his servant contrived for me a bath, a change of clothes—those of a full private—and a breakfast of kidney and bacon ! As I changed and ate, D.A.D.O.S. told me how the back areas had suffered from the night-long bombardment. Our Divisional Staff had speedily been driven out of their conspicuous château Headquarters and, more serious by far, details such as the motor-supply column, the mobile veterinary section, and the divisional canteen had been trapped in Fismes and suffered very heavily. Fismes was the most important centre in the forward area and housed the big Expeditionary Force canteen as well as the details of two divisions. It had accordingly been pelted with heavy shells all night. For once I felt less envious of the lot of those whom Colonel Page had a month earlier referred to as " officials of the rearward services." A little over an hour later, feeling drier and happier but rather groggy about the knees, I returned to the war, reporting to the Brigadier, who was by that time trying to organise a defensive line on the rising ground below Roucy village.

HIGH GROUND

III

HIGH GROUND

It was then I found how terribly the Brigade had suffered. Hardly a hundred had won back across the river. There were Lowry, the young C.O. of the West Yorkshires with a bullet wound in his foot, and his adjutant, Sanders ; a corporal of the same regiment ; a handful of the Middlesex ; two or three of the Devons, and a few gunners.

It was difficult to get a clear picture of the attack. This had been so violent and our trenches so thinly held that all organised resistance on our divisional front had been at once overwhelmed. But the chief danger had come apparently from the flanking movements, helped as these were by the pronounced salient we were holding. The enemy had carried the strong French positions on the Chemin des Dames after a fierce but short assault, and at the same time under cover of the very heavy mist—the sure shield of the German offensives—and helped by the sparse nature of the trench garrison, had worked his way up the Miette stream on the right. Indeed, the advance on this flank was so rapid that small groups of Germans were across the Aisne near the Bois de Gernicourt before the remnants of the 23rd Brigade had been collected at Pontavert (how providential, I reflected, that I had never got there !), but even before this fact had become known it was evident that any attempt to hold the line of the river with the few survivors was quite unthinkable.

The 25th Division had been moved up overnight and was now being doled out along the whole length of the IXth Corps front, one brigade to each of the divisions in line—the 7th Brigade to the 21st Division, the 75th to the 8th, and the 74th to the 50th. The 21st Division had been on the flank of the main German thrust, and had not yet, relatively speaking, been heavily engaged, but both the 8th and 50th Divisions had ceased to exist as fighting formations.

As regards the 8th, it is doubtful if the total strength of all ranks who succeeded in getting back across the river was more than a few hundred, and while the other two brigades had both suffered as heavily as we had, their staffs had even worse experiences. The 24th Brigade had been surrounded and bombed in their Headquarters and, although more by good luck than good management most of them had managed to escape, Wimble, their Staff Captain, had been taken prisoner and Brigadier-General R. Haig sufficiently gassed to prevent his taking any further part in the battle. The 25th had suffered still more heavily—both the Brigadier, General Husey, and Pascoe, his young Brigade-Major, being missing. They had only been appointed to their respective posts a week or two previously, and now all that was known of their fate was that the General had been seen on the bridge at Berry-au-Bac sick unto death in the throes of gas-poisoning, and Pascoe rallying the remnants of the Brigade in a despairing effort to arrest the enemy onrush.[1]

---

[1] *Both were later reported killed.*

The command of what was left of the 8th Divisional Infantry accordingly passed to Brigadier-General Grogan, and from this point the story of the 8th Division is identified with that of the 23rd Brigade.

The arrival of welcome reinforcements in the shape of the 75th Brigade and some 650 men of all units from the Divisional Lewis-Gun School made it possible for some sort of defensive line to be organised in front of Roucy village. It is an eloquent commentary on French Staff work that such large numbers of men had been withdrawn from trench duties for training on the advice of the Higher Command that no hostile attack was to be expected ! It was not until 11 a.m. that a line was established and a large gap was then found to exist on the left flank where the remnants of the 50th Division should have touched the French. How those Frenchmen must have " legged it " !

By this time the barrage had died down, though German high-velocity guns kept up steady long-range shelling of the back areas. Viewed from the hills above the village the area of operations presented a vivid spectacle. The day was extremely hot, the sunshine brilliant, and, but for the deep drone of heavy shells winging their way rearwards, all sounds of battle were temporarily stilled. Below, the steep green slopes showed few signs of activity save where in the fields and gardens round Roucy little groups of khaki figures moved busily about. The Aisne and its attendant canal glittered like silver ribbons in the sun, but in the vacated trench area beyond hung a pall of haze and dust, which lifting at intervals revealed the roads thick with marching regiments in field grey, with guns, lorries, and wagons. Above, like great unwinking eyes, rode observation balloons, towed along by motor transport.

On no other occasion in the Great War did the Germans so rapidly follow up their assault, and battalions advanced in fours across our captured trenches even before the last defenders had been overcome.

What a target the whole scene presented! What havoc even a few eighteen-pounders would have worked on those crowded roads! But not a gun of either the 8th or 50th Divisional Artillery had been got across the river. The 110th R.A. Brigade of the 25th Division which had taken up positions on the low ground south of the Aisne, was practically wiped out by 9 a.m., and the 112th Brigade, though more fortunate, was only able to keep a few guns in action until the afternoon. Moreover, many bridges across the river at Ponta-vert, Concevreux, and Maizy had not been destroyed in time. Consequently, not only was it impossible for us to engage the enemy until he had come within rifle range, but he was enabled to move his guns and transport across the river without let or hindrance.

By midday German infantry had crossed both canal and river in force—at Maizy on the left and at Pontavert in the centre—but not till between 2 and 3 p.m. did any attack develop. Large numbers then advanced in open order on a front of about two miles. They were met with heavy rifle and machine-gun fire and, unsupported as they were by artillery, suffered severe casualties without piercing the defence. But it was not long before the gaps in our line were probed, and working rapidly round our left flank the enemy forced us to make a precipitate retirement to the crest of the Roucy hills.

All the heavily fortified positions prepared by the French in the woods above the village had to be abandoned, and the new line was taken up astride the Roucy-Ventelay road, where although cover, either natural or artificial, was scanty, the field of fire was excellent.

By this time enemy aerial activity had considerably developed, and low-lying planes machine-gunned the roads with unpleasant regularity. The observation balloons had come much nearer and against the clear sky looked startlingly close—one heated Cockney of the Middlesex guaranteeing that " 'e could spit into the barsket from 'ere—easy ! "

In a ditch shelter by the side of the road the officers of Brigade Headquarters gathered for the first time since dinner the night before, and appropriately enough for the first food they had, with the exception of myself, touched since—and I kept very quiet about my breakfast ! It was not a very sumptuous repast, consisting only of one tin of sausages divided between eight of us, and eaten off one penknife. It was also regrettable that Thompson, the thoughtful contributor of the tin, was not there when it was opened and so got no share of its contents.

Perhaps it was well that the meal was not a heavier one, for we were allowed little respite to digest it, and at about 5.30 p.m. the Germans attempted to storm our positions. Lines of infantry emerged from the cover of the woods in extended

order, cheering and shouting, but their advance
was halted by a steady volume of rifle and machine-
gun fire. The check was short-lived, for the gap
on our left must by this time have been some miles
in width. Taking full advantage of this, the enemy
began a turning movement, at the same time as he
subjected the front to a bombardment from the
trench-mortars which he had been quick to bring
up in support of his infantry. These tactics were
employed throughout his advance. The front
would be pinned down by trench-mortar fire, while
small groups of infantry with light machine-guns
would dribble round in twos and threes ; and,
taking advantage of depressions in the ground and
any natural cover, endeavour to turn the flanks of
the position. The German Army might have
favoured mass-formation attacks at the Kaiser
Manœuvre or in the early days of 1914–15, but they
had learnt well and truly since then, and between the
Aisne and the Marne, 1918, gave us as fine an
object lesson in open warfare and the use of cover
as the most academic Aldershot staff-officer could
have desired.

The situation swiftly became critical. It was
obvious that we could not hope to hold our positions
against even a frontal attack if this were pressed
energetically and supported by covering fire. Yet our
left flank was already turned, and there was now every
danger that the rapidity of the German penetration up
the valley from Maizy to Meurival would cut off our
line of retreat. The only small satisfaction that we
could draw from the enemy's tactics was that they
gave us a much-needed breather, but this I was not
privileged to enjoy. Instead I was dispatched on a

signaller's push-bike to carry a message to 8th Divisional Headquarters at Montigny, the road to which led through the area of the transport lines and camps which the night before had sheltered the stores, canteens, regimental details, and other impedimenta of the Division. Now only deserted, shell-swept ruins were left, and the road was strewn with the bodies of man and horse, with charred limbers and splintered wagons, destroyed as they had striven to escape. This damage, I registered with relief, had all been done some hours before, and shells were no longer falling in the vicinity, so that there was no desperate need for haste. This was a blessing, for I found a G.S. pedal cycle a heavy vehicle to propel at speed, and I was very weary. Also I had since morning had a queer feeling that all the muscles of my stomach had turned to cold water, and my legs become unsteady —sensations I put down to the gas I must have inhaled. Reaching Montigny I found that the G.O.C. and most of the Staff had moved still farther back, but duly delivered my message and got a lift back in a Staff car which was being sent up to fetch Major Roupell, the G.S.O. II. The car stopped to pick him up on the roadside a few hundred yards short of the crest of the ridge near where we had eaten our sausages. The road had then been clear and untouched. Now the shallow blast of a whizz-bang marked the metalled crown. Ten yards farther something twisted and shapeless which had once been a man, had been blown like a bundle of old brown paper on to the grass. The sight gave me a shock. I had seen many corpses that day, but this one was different. It had not been there half an hour before, and it said as plainly as any signpost, " This road is still dangerous." I was seized with a desire to get off it, so that I was relieved on reporting my return to be told I was to go back with Roupell and help Parsloe, who had been out of all this, to get the Brigade transport away before it too might be entrapped.

The day began to wane and the glow of the sunset was dimmed by the rolling clouds of smoke which rose from blazing villages, farmsteads, and huts. The coming of night was welcome indeed, and in the gathering dusk the scattered line of defenders was hastily withdrawn, a few men at a time, until by the time that darkness had fallen new positions had been taken up on the ridge above Montigny between Les Grands Savarts and Romain which was burning fiercely. This withdrawal was not, I learnt later, accomplished without collisions with the more pushful German patrols, whose advance turned out to be so rapid on the right that they captured our entire 25th Field Ambulance in Bouvancourt, surrounding the village before its occupants had any idea they were in danger. Colonel G. J. Ormsby, the A.D.M.S., had come up in a small Ford ambulance to warn them to retire. He was actually entering the village when some one challenged him. He took no notice, and the next thing he knew was that a burst of machine-gun fire had been opened on him at short range.

He got a bullet through his arm, but his chauffeur, with great presence of mind, turned the wheels full lock, spun round and carried him off before any further hurt came to the car or its occupants.

The officer commanding the ambulance, Lieut.-Colonel T. P. Puddicombe, was pounced on in the village street by Germans who mistook his rank for that of a sergeant ; and eventually marched off in charge of an escort of one, and he an Alsatian. Suddenly some blessed British or French machine-gunner opened a burst of fire on the roadway. Prisoner and escort dived simultaneously for cover, Puddicombe making a wild dash to get off the road, only to land in a swamp, into which he at once sank up to his waist. There, in the bright moon-light, he had to stay for over an hour, crouched in a clump of bullrushes, the chilly water breast high, while the Alsatian hunted him, Germans moved around him on the road and on the high ground, and the Allied machine - gunner intermittently sprayed the swamp with machine-gun bullets. Providentially he was neither found nor hit, and as soon as he judged that his escort had given up the hunt he emerged. Then started a long crawl on hands and knees through the enemy picket line, a very laborious and painful process in his cramped and sodden state, but once clear of the sentry-posts, whose position he could fix from their voices, he up and fled, *homo erectus* once more, into Montigny which he found still in British hands.

I found the transport picketed in a large wood in which stood some old French hutments. Whereas the British Army with its greater resources would have built such habitations of iron-elephant shelters or properly carpentered planking, all very G.S. and efficient, the French were frequently obliged to make up slenderer resources by skilled crafts-manship. Whoever made these huts must have been a trained woodsman and something of an artist, for they were all constructed of roughly trimmed poles, fitting exactly into their surroundings and giving the effect of a camp of rustic-work summer-houses. This homely, tranquil effect was heightened by the soft twilight and the music of the horse-lines, the lazy swish of tails, and the reflective champing of bits. I was suddenly conscious of a great longing to rest, threw myself on a wire bed, and on the instant was asleep. But not for long. Within the hour, Parsloe had shaken me into consciousness. It was dark and the transport was moving.

Night had laid a cool hand across the fevered countryside, masking the ugliness, toning down the racket of the day, and distilling sweet scents from dew-drenched earth and foliage. Man might strive mightily to make night a second day, to keep the fires of destruction stoked up to the same pressure throughout the twenty-four hours, but he might never wholly succeed. There was always a spell during the hours of darkness when Nature called a halt, enforcing a relaxation of effort if not a complete lull. So now, although overhead long-range shells slid or rumbled, according to their calibre, bursting dully far away in the rear, they sounded less angry, more deliberate ; and although all around were movement and wakefulness, the strained watching of the troops in line, the anxious haste of drivers to get their lorries, wagons, limbers, or cookers clear of the fighting zone, the fact that only those close at hand could be seen had the effect of lowering the tension.

Once the transport was out of the wood and fairly

launched upon the road it was engulfed in the spate of retreating columns from other brigades and divisions. The congestion looked almost hopeless— so much my mind registered and no more. It was too tired to function and that night march remains a blur in my memory, a medley of wagon-wheels turning and gritting, legs of horses and men moving, regularly, regularly, stopping, then moving again ; of shouts and curses and distant flashes out of the darkness. All night long the columns crawled slowly back, toiling up steep hillsides and pounding down sudden valleys : the march ever and again interrupted by the crash of a shell, squeals of wounded animals, an abrupt halt—then on again. As a matter for history, the speed of the German advance, his accurate long-range fire on road junctions and bridges, the convergence of routes, the hilly nature of the country, and the heavy casualties to man and beast ; these combined to make the saving of the transport a matter of great difficulty, and it says much for the discipline and devotion of those concerned that the almost impossible was accomplished.

THE VESLE

me, one Sheriff, a stocky, bull-necked, gypsy-looking Cockney. In the course of the March retreat Sheriff had " scrounged " a hen, which had since travelled round with the West Yorkshire transport, perched up on one of the G.S. wagons, in an improvised coop. This worthy fowl had not forgotten her duties during the agitations of the night, and had duly laid her regular egg, which, fried to a turn, was now presented to " Hinchers " on his bacon. The rest of us had to be content with bacon and fried bread, and even that we were not allowed to consume at our ease. Indeed we had scarcely swallowed it when some one shouted that he could see the infantry on the far side of the river falling back. Almost simultaneously an alert enemy gunner spotted us and began a brisk burst of shelling—a sharp reminder that we were still within range and should therefore have chosen a less conspicuous place to halt. The first salvos luckily went wide, but before we could limber up, throw cooking-pots on to the nearest wagon and make off, one better-aimed burst on the road beside us, seriously wounding two men. Before the smoke had cleared, a dishevelled private, tin-hat ludicrously over one eye and blood streaming from a deep scratch on his grimy face, dashed up to me. It was Mr. Parkin—" Bob " Parkin from Rotherham, steel worker and public-house bookie in civilian life—who seized my hand. " Ba goom, sir," he gasped, " I am glad to see thee ! I thowt thou was deeäd when I didn't see thee leave t' dug-outs ! " In a sense it was a reproof, a reminder that, so much had I been intent on self-preservation during the past twenty-four hours, I had given never a thought to my servant's fate, although he, good soul, had been concerned for mine. It was a welcome reunion, though there was no time to do more than acknowledge the fact and trot along to catch up the column disappearing over the brow of the hill.

It is not pertinent to this narrative to follow the transport farther for the moment. Suffice it to say that throughout the long summer day, cursing, sweating men urged tired and frightened animals rearwards along crowded, dusty roads under a blazing sun. By way of Vendeuil, Savigny, Faverolles —I remember reflecting whether this was the origin of the breed of poultry of that name—Lhery, and Romigny we went, harassed by enemy aeroplanes and goaded by the knowledge that the front was falling back as fast behind us. As the sun began to lose its power we reached a temporary haven of refuge on a wooded slope above the remains of the village of Jonquery. Here we decided to halt for the night. It was a lovely spot, the woods shining with silver birches and the golden tassels of laburnum, and below the green ruins of the village, which only dated from 1914 yet were now as mellow and as venerable as those of any time-hallowed monastery or castle.

I had imagined that all my kit had gone west at Bois des Buttes, but Parkin produced from the Headquarters wagon an entirely unauthorised piece of luggage in the shape of a large wooden box which carried all sorts of odds and ends of personal equipment and possessions. There was a silver concert flute picked up in some village on the Somme, two or three prehistoric flint arrowheads, and a short three-barrelled curiosity of a shot-gun which I had found in a deserted house near Amiens. There was also, and this was much more welcome, a complete set of service-dress, jacket, boots, puttees, breeches, and a shirt to take the place of the tickly "grey-back" and private soldier's uniform, in which D.A.D.O.S. had rigged me out. There was, alas, no spare shaving tackle, but these were soon borrowed from Hinchcliffe, and in a reasonably short space of time I both felt and looked a new man. The cool of the evening, a whisky and water, and one or more of Parkin's woodbines before turning in, and presto ! how far away had receded the heat and anxiety of the day.

To return now to the battle-front. During the small hours of the morning the Germans had suddenly attacked our line from the direction of Bouvancourt and, breaking through on the right, forced the scattered defenders on the Montigny heights to beat a hasty retreat towards the Vesle, where another position was taken up in front of Jonchery. This was the movement we had seen beginning just before we were shelled. General Grogan had then been ordered to collect what stragglers he could in the neighbourhood of Jonchery and with them to hold the south bank of the river. At the same time the G.O.C. 75th Brigade had been instructed to fill the gap to the right and join up with the 21st Division. By some marvel of improvisation, this was done and a line established by daylight from where the Prouilly road crosses the Vesle to a large farm about one and a half miles north-west of Jonchery.

Dawn on the 28th therefore saw the situation temporarily retrieved so far as the remnants of the

8th, 50th, and the greater part of the 25th Divisions were concerned, and the morning wore slowly on without any further enemy action manifesting itself. As the sun climbed high into a cloudless sky, it beat down the more fiercely upon a panorama which looked strangely peaceful at first sight, although the roads smoked with the passage of troops and transport, and here and there burning farmsteads glowed dully in the brilliant sunshine.

While the enemy remained quiescent, feverish efforts were made to consolidate the position against his next assault. Touch was again established on both flanks, and although the line was exceedingly " sketchy," it was some satisfaction to know that it was again more or less continuous. On the right the 21st Division, despite heavy casualties, was still able to maintain an organised front and was in touch with the French on its farther flank. On the left the situation was far less reassuring. Here, towards the centre of his main stroke, the enemy advance had been even more rapid and a deep salient had been driven into the Allied line, the disintegration of which was complete. Moreover, by now the survivors of the 8th and 50th Divisions and the French who had been rushed up to their support were well and truly mixed up, which meant that somewhere behind, and a long way behind, three divisional commanders were nominally responsible for the same sector ! It was on the left flank that the next blow fell, and shortly after noon a determined attack was launched against the front held by remnants of the 50th Division about two miles to the west of Jonchery. So vigorous was this onslaught that the line gave, and the enemy, pushing through the gap with great rapidity, began to work his way towards the high wooded ridges above Vendeuil. The attack was simultaneously extended towards the right, forcing a hasty retreat across the Vesle along the whole front held by the British Corps.

All the morning's work of consolidation had been for nothing, and as the tired khaki figures struggled up the steep slopes south of the river, they could see enemy artillery and transport pouring in continuous streams down the two roads converging on Jonchery, while their infantry swarmed busily across the open country. It was a sight given to gunners only in dreams, but now not a gun was available.

On the crest of the hills overlooking the river, along the Jonchery-Branscourt road, was an old French strongpoint, and here a stand was made for about two hours. It was a wonderful position commanding the passage of the river, and from it machine-guns and rifles took a steady toll of the advancing swarms in field-grey. Once again the frontal attack was halted and for a time the enemy remained discreetly out of effective range. The check was not of long duration as little opposition was offered on either flank, and German patrols, plentifully provided with light machine-guns, occupied the high ground west of Jonchery towards Vendeuil about 4 p.m.

The position was soon so nearly surrounded as to be untenable, and towards five o'clock it was hastily vacated, its defenders falling back under fire towards the crest running almost parallel with and to the east of the main Jonchery-Savigny road. Here some old practice trenches furnished very welcome cover, and by the strenuous personal

Previous page: "There is much wire."
German trench-mortar team passing the old 8th Division front line near Berry-au-Bac.

Above: "Everywhere was ruin."
Our captured positions on the Aisne Canal seen from Hill 108. Berry-au-Bac in the background.

Right: The Bridge at Pontavert.
German infantry being ferried across the Aisne. The vital crossings were seized within three hours of the opening assault.

Left: German infantry advancing across the battle zone.

Above: "By way of Savigny . . . we went."
French and British troops at Savigny, May 28th.
(Note signpost to Jonchery.)

Following page: "By now French and British were well and truly
mixed up."

Previous page: "Their infantry swarmed across the open country."
German machine-gun detachment approaching the River Vesle.

Above: "Crugny was already in German hands."
German transport approaching Crugny (in distance).

Opposite above: In the Open. British infantry awaiting the enemy.
May 29th.

Opposite below: In the Open. German infantry in the unspoilt country
on May 27th.

Left: "Two-way traffic congestion of the worst kind."
8th Divisional infantry, French infantry, transport, and cookers at
Passy, May 29th.

Above: They remembered 1870. Refugees crossing the Marne at
Reuil.

Following page: Refugees and retreating French troops at Chatillon.

Previous page: The last handful. 8th Divisional infantry crossing the Marne.

Above: Prisoners. Men of the West Yorkshires being marched back.

Below: Prisoners. First British prisoners being brought back through a mine crater.

Above: The Winterberg (Californie Plateau) after its capture.

Below: Field Marshal von Hindenburg and H.I.M. the Kaiser on the Winterberg, May 28th.

Right: "The Headquarters of the 150th Brigade were taken and the Brigadier made prisoner."

Left: The Kaiser talking to the captured Brigadier. With H.I.M. are Generals von Böhn and von Conta.

efforts of Grogan and Millis, the heterogeneous collection of tired troops, representing almost every unit of three divisions, artillery as well as infantry, was again formed into some coherent line. Close by on the left was a large farmstead occupied by a handful of French infantry, but on the far side of the road the ground sloped upwards towards a great mass of woods. That these were already in German possession was obvious from the grey-clad figures that from time to time could be seen moving among the trees, but in spite of this the General wisely decided that every effort would have to be made to prevent the enemy from securing the Jonchery-Savigny road, as the longer use of this was denied him the more effectively would his main advance be delayed. A party of about seventy men, under Major Cope of the 2nd Devons and Thompson was accordingly sent forward to take up a position on the far side of the road and to check any German attempt to debouch from the woods.

As it was not known how many of the enemy were already concealed in the undergrowth and cornfields between the woods and the road, which, by the way, were nowhere more than a hundred yards apart, the task of this party was not an enviable one, although actually their antics provided a little much-needed comic relief. They made the short advance in copy-book style, in extended order, and finished up with a truly ferocious bayonet charge through a large cornfield, out of which several Germans scuttled like bolting rabbits. No blood was shed on either side in this operation !

The party took up their position in the cornfields between the road and the woods, from the cover of which the enemy made no further attempt to deploy, although he kept up a desultory rifle fire until dusk. Then two round heads in coal-scuttle helmets popped up inquisitively from some bushes about a hundred yards from the post. Their owners, realising at once that they had come too far for the good of their health, bobbed down and began to crawl away. Unfortunately for them their movements had been observed by the watchful Thompson. Pointing the retreating pair out to the man nearest him—a sergeant of the 1st Sherwood Foresters—he remarked, in much the same tones as one would use to a waiter, " Sergeant, shoot me those Boche ! " " Very good, sir," came the perfectly composed answer, two quick shots, and those two Germans were no more. Whereupon Thompson promptly marched out and rifled the bodies of the slain, gaining valuable identification and also, what was of more immediate importance, matches !

The coming of darkness rendered the isolated position of the party still more precarious, but throughout the night they kept up a perfectly astounding pandemonium and a great deal of rifle-fire. Whether the bluff succeeded, or whether the enemy were equally tired, or both, it is impossible to say, but the fact was that no further hostile action developed.

Meanwhile, on the slopes about Jonquery all was not rest and quiet, and as soon as daylight waned, quartermasters, wonderful men, made ready to take rations up the line. Business as usual, whatever the circumstances, was the quartermasters' motto, but this was now a hard thing for drivers and animals concerned. They were indeed very nearly "all-in" after their two days of forced marching, and were now at least three times the normal distance behind the front, yet although the usual grouses were to be heard as the men got ready —"Why the blinking 'ell couldn't we have dumped rations on the way?" "'Ow can I ask these perishing mules o' mine to go back and shake 'ands with Jerry again?" and many more less printable— the ration limbers set out at nightfall to do the whole long journey twice again. That must have been a weary pilgrimage along strange roads in the dark. Several times they lost their way, once turning back when almost into Crugny, which was already in German hands, but they got there at last and dumped their precious loads on the roadside a few hundred yards behind the ridge which our troops were holding.

As he rode on ahead to report to the Brigadier, Parsloe was in the mood to congratulate himself for finding his way so successfully, and also on his good luck in avoiding capture in collisions with the enemy. He anticipated a word of commendation. Instead he found a very cold, hungry, and irate General huddled up in a length of trench trying to snatch a little sleep, and was heartily cursed for leaving rations on the roadside. Why the blank blank couldn't he have brought them right up to the firing line? Weren't the troops tired enough without having to hunt for food which others were too idle to bring up to them? And so on. In extenuation it must be remembered that officers and men had had practically no food and less sleep for forty-eight hours of hard fighting; also that the nights were as cold as the days were hot—ample excuse surely for ragged tempers.

It was daylight before the ration parties returned, Parsloe bringing an order from the Brigadier that I should join him with the officers' chargers and the Brigade grooms.

THE RIDGES

V

THE RIDGES

ALONG the whole battle-line the night of May 28–29 had passed quietly and uneventfully. However much it was to the Germans' advantage to keep up the pressure and to allow the defenders no rest in which to recuperate or reorganise, factors were now combining to enforce a standstill at nights.

There was the tactical factor ; that with their line making a deep pocket into strange country, hilly and wooded, the Germans would be mad to hazard night operations. There was the supply factor ; that already they must have been in danger of out-distancing their rations and ammunition. There was lastly the personal factor ; that the human machine needs recharging. Not only was there physical fatigue, but the reaction now succeeding the nervous energy and excitement which had keyed up attackers and attacked for over two days. In those two days the Germans had burst clean through a highly organised section of the allied line, through the reserve and emergency positions behind it, and had poured ten miles into the rich, open country of the Champagne. It was already an astonishing feat of arms, and in itself sufficient reason why a quiet night should not have been surprising.

But no matter how quiet he might be, the enemy

was too close and his intentions too little known for Grogan's men to allow themselves the luxury of a decent " kip " ; though the restorative effect of only a few hours' semi-wakeful dozing, undisturbed and unattacked, enabled them to start the day of May 29 somewhat refreshed in body and lighter in spirit. Which was as well, for the Germans were up betimes, seemingly determined to " make a day of it."

Just as the first glow of dawn began to gild the horizon, large bodies of infantry issued confidently from the dark mass of the woods in the belief, apparently, that Cope's advance party had been withdrawn. A fierce gust of rifle-fire sharply disillusioned them and they doubled hastily back to cover.

This was about 3.30 a.m., after which hour no further overt action took place for some time, although it was obvious that a more determined move was impending for which the enemy was massing in the woods. In spite of this, Cope's little party vigorously kept up its ridiculous bluff until nearly 11 a.m., when strong parties of Germans were seen working round both flanks. Then, and not till they were in imminent danger of being entirely surrounded, was the order given to fall back and rejoin the main body on the far side of the road. This, needless to say, was obeyed with alacrity, and the mere handful of troops, which by sheer bluff had held up an overwhelming number of the enemy since the previous afternoon, fled precipitately back to the ridge behind. Immediately their withdrawal was observed, Germans swarmed out after them, opening a furious fusillade from rifles and machine-guns without, however, doing any serious damage.

This time the enemy meant business, and with much shouting and cheering advanced to the assault of the main position. For a time he was held, but his weight of numbers soon began to tell, until about noon Grogan saw the fruitlessness of further resistance and ordered a general retirement, a few men at a time (" retirement by platoons " gives quite the wrong impression as all formations had long since disappeared) on to another ridge which was humped in front of Treslon village about a mile in rear. This withdrawal was detected by the enemy and was not effected without difficulty or casualties, but once again the Brigadier by his energy and personal example extracted order out of chaos, and some sort of line was formed. It was at this juncture that I arrived with the chargers.

By this time the force under Grogan's command had become pitifully thin—a ragged army of Falstaffian dimensions. And what a collection ! The General himself ; his Brigade Staff-officers ; Smythe, the G.S.O. III., 8th Division ; Major Cope of the 2nd Devons ; Colonel Moore of the 1st Sherwood Foresters, the only infantry C.O. of the 8th Division not already a casualty ; two colonels of the 50th Division without a single man of the units they once commanded ; a knot of machine-gunners from the same division whose gun refused to function from lack of water ; a woeful sprinkling of all units of the 8th and most of the 25th and 50th Divisions ; a total of perhaps two hundred and fifty—all hungry, sleepless, dirty ; many bleeding from wounds of greater or less severity. A number of khaki-clad French colonial troops, part of a division which had just come up as reinforcements, completed the tale of men.

This scattered remnant was disposed along a steep ridge, deep in growing corn, which sloped away towards the left into the wooded valley of the Ardre. Here, among the trees which bordered the river were more French, blue-clad " poilus " as well as khaki-clad colonials, chattering and laughing and making great play with their Hotchkiss automatic rifles against German planes. In rear the hillside sloped abruptly down to a miniature valley in which nestled the village of Treslon and at whose farther side the ground rose sharply up to another ridge of a more wooded nature, which I will call the Bouleuse ridge, from its proximity to the village of that name.

I had not chosen a very enjoyable moment to arrive, for the enemy had just elected to turn his machine-guns on to the ridge in an attempt at barrage-fire. The air hummed with bullets. Bullets scythed shrilly through the standing corn : kicked vicious spurts of dust from the sun-baked earth. Ricochets whined angrily away overhead. Fortunately the fire was very inaccurate and did little actual damage to the scattered force lying flattened to earth along the crest of the ridge.

Weary and hungry as they were, the spirits of the little band were astonishing. This was due very largely to the example set by the General. He had not had the patience to wait for his own charger, but had during the morning commandeered two horses belonging to a gunner F.O.O., who had paid a visit to the firing line. One of these had already been killed. He was now riding his second, and in a position of extreme personal and tactical danger as he was, after three days of continuous fighting, he bumped joyously up and down the line—his round, shiny face wreathed in smiles, his eyes twinkling, chuckling to himself as if the whole affair were a species of boyish joke.

His borrowed steed was soon wounded ; no matter, his own horses had arrived. Mounting himself on " Sandy," his pet pony, a cobby, bob-tailed chestnut, he resumed his ride in full view of the enemy, talking and joking with the men as he passed, all the time affectionately belabouring " Sandy " with his great crook-handled walking-stick.

This may sound like bravado, but it was not. Despite the bold face he put on before the men, Grogan was fully conscious of the seriousness of the situation, and quietly took what steps he could to meet it. Word had been sent that the 19th British Division were being rushed up, and that one battalion should at any moment come into position behind us on the Bouleuse ridge. Very prudently he would not rely on this support being forthcoming in time, and surreptitiously sent back a picked handful of his command to act as a covering party, when the next inevitable retirement should take place. Me he sent down into Treslon village to discover the headquarters of a French regiment believed to be there, and to ask their commanding officer if he would conform to our dispositions and contribute a few men to strengthen the very inadequate covering force.

I eventually found the French comfortably ensconced in a cellar, very much at their ease. They did not show themselves very pleased to see me, and my message they received with frank incredulity. What, barked the Colonel, there was an English General in the firing-line? One asked him to believe that? Impossible! Only the prompt evidence of an eye-witness, a " sous-officier " who entered the cellar at that moment and exclaimed, " But yes, my Colonel, there is ! A mad English General on horseback ! I have seen him ! " convinced him that I was not lying. Even so he politely but firmly declined to support us in any way.

Cursing all Frenchmen, I went back to the ridge only to find Millis equally vehement. Apparently the colonials on our left were without officers and threatened to decamp, proclaiming loudly that they were only supposed to be " en soutien " and not in the front line. It was only by repeated journeys to them and earnest cajoling that Millis had so far succeeded in getting them to stay their ground.

The arrival of an S.A.A. limber in the valley behind was most welcome as ammunition was running short. Ledward and the grooms and I proceeded to distribute this on horseback. Taking as many bandoliers as we could carry on one arm we galloped up the hill and along the line, whooping and laughing, throwing one or two to each man ; then galloped back for more. It was exciting while it lasted, the excitement of rapid action, something dashing to revel in instead of the usual long ordeal to endure. The exhilaration of movement banished all sense of danger, and though we showed up against the skyline as against a sight-screen, I found myself concerned only to check my horse from stumbling.

The whole scene, its sunny fields of waving corn, its galloping horsemen, was more reminiscent of some old-time battle picture than an episode from the Great War ; and in spite of the pressing attention of machine-gun bullets, I was carried back to field days on Laffan's Plain or the Long Valley. But such distant memories were destined to be rudely shattered. The reason for the German inactivity was soon apparent, when groups of infantry were seen to be manhandling into position several heavy trench-mortars, the real " minen-werfers." Owing to the weight of these pieces and their ammunition it was some time before they were ready to open fire, but at about 3 p.m. an aimed bombardment started which in an entrenched position would have been serious enough, but which no troops, however fresh, or however high their morale, could have long withstood in the open. The effect of these great shells, two-hundred-pound steel canisters of high explosive, on the iron-hard soil was terrible, the tearing crash of the burst as demoralising as the execution wrought by the long, flying splinters. The little red-tiled houses in Treslon crumbled in columns of black dust. Men were torn to bleeding shreds. The line quickly thinned.

I was standing holding my mare, Peggy, and talking to Millis who was mounted, when a minen-werfer landed too close to us to be comfortable. With a sharp hiss, a splinter flew between us. I looked down at my jacket. Millis asked, " Are you hit ? " " No," I answered, somewhat sobered by what I had seen, " but look here ! " There was a four-inch hole *in* through my jacket just behind the right pocket, and another *out again in front of it.* There was no mark on my breeches. An inch nearer and my leg would have been shattered at the hip.

On the instant I realised what a mess there would be if Peggy were hit. I could not bear to think of it, so walked her down to a gravel pit which stood half-way up the slope and tethered her to a hawthorn. She was not to be there for long, but for the moment I was happier without her.

The worst was now to come. On the left the French again grew restive, and Millis started off once more to rally them. Close beside me Prance was snatching an odd meal of dry bread, bully beef, and vintage champagne in the saddle, but seeing Millis set off, shouted, " Hang it all ! Wait a moment for a fellow ! I'm coming too ! " Handing the bottle to his servant, he galloped off after Millis across the ridge. At that moment the General told me to go back to the Bouleuse ridge where a field telephone was now working, and tell 8th Division to send some ambulances up at once. I had just returned from sending this message when I was shocked to see Millis, his face dead white, his uniform soaked in blood, being helped down by two men. " Got it in both ankles. Prance was killed," he told me. " Can you lend me your horse ? " And so, because the ambulances would take time to reach us, I fetched Peggy. Millis was helped on to her back and, supported by an orderly, was led from the scene on the long road which led to Blighty.

Then I heard what had happened. He and Prance had not ridden more than fifty yards towards the left when a minenwerfer shell burst plumb between them, killing both horses and Prance instantaneously. Millis had escaped with a wound through his ankles, but his hurt looked worse than it was because he had fallen in his horse's blood.

The moral effect of this blow was out of all proportion to its practical significance. Among so many casualties, these two seemed to mark a turning-point. Looking back on that afternoon through the reversed telescope of the years, it is not difficult to see why. Up to that time our little family at Brigade Headquarters had come through unscathed. Then, in the twinkling of an eye, an irreparable gap had been made. The sun seemed to go in. In no one was the effect more noticeable than the General, and again his attitude was contagious.

The breaking-point was being reached, both individually and tactically. The pitiless bombardment continued. Colonel Moore was killed. To complete the utter hopelessness of the situation, Allied guns, whether French or British, began shelling the ridge. The first salvo, all too accurately aimed, burst well in the middle of the tired line, doing fearful havoc. One man was lifted off his feet and blown clean through the stunted hedge.

It was my job again to struggle sweating up the steep hillside to the telephone, and beg the people behind, some one, any one, to put a stop to such murder. Noting with some relief that the expected reinforcements had arrived and the 2nd Wiltshires were in position, I came back to the valley where I found that Bourdillon had arrived with three ambulances.

A vivid picture stands out in my mind of that moment. From the ridge in front, mutilated human beings, Englishmen and French, were being carried down on hurdles or ground-sheets—such medical amenities as stretchers had disappeared long before. Bourdillon bent over to talk to one poor devil whose stomach had been ripped open, his entrails only held in by the sopping first field dressing. He came across to me. " I can't take him on the cars," he said, as if in apology ; " he's bound to die, and it would only mean pushing some one off who might recover. If there weren't so many men about I'd do what he is asking me." " What's that ? " I asked. " Shoot him, and put him out of pain ! " As he spoke, the bombardment quickened to rapid fire—stopped suddenly. There was a harsh rattle of musketry, shrill blasts on whistles, a rush of khaki figures down the hillside. The General and Ledward galloped past. The ambulances clattered off down the valley in a cloud of dust. The Treslon ridge was in German hands. They were firing at us as we ran back. A half-limber drawn by two mules pounded past me up the slope. I jumped for the tailboard, felt something hit me, thump ! in the small of the back. I fell off, picked myself up, ran on and threw myself down breathless behind the bushes on the ridge-top. Was I wounded ? I felt myself gingerly, withdrew my hand. There was no blood. I fetched a sign of relief. Still, I had been hit by something, either a spent bullet or a piece of hard earth thrown up by a bullet, for I carried a painful bruise for some days.

If at other times the enemy had been slow in following up his advantage, he lost no time now. The assault which had carried the Treslon ridge was allowed to lose none of its momentum. Even as the attackers paused to re-form, they brought their numerous light machine-guns into play upon the survivors of the mixed force as they scrambled to cover on the Bouleuse ridge. Then, urged on by the loud shouts of their non-commissioned officers, the Germans swept forward in pursuit. Before we had had time to regain our breath, much less to rally, German signal lights were rising from the thickets on the slope just in front of us. Worse still, one enemy post actually succeeded in reaching a clump of bushes on the crest of the ridge itself.

This called for prompt and energetic action. Calling to him about a dozen men and a young officer of the 2nd East Lancashires, the Brigadier, still mounted on Sandy, led them at the charge straight at the thicket. When the party were a few yards away a German infantryman stood up and fired his rifle point-blank at the General. Luckily he was no marksman and the only sufferer was poor Sandy hit through the soft, fleshy part of his nose. With a total disregard for the desperateness of the situation as well as for the niceties of military etiquette, the General signalled the miss by "cocking a snook" at the astonished German! Then leaving him and his friends to be dealt with by the others, he coolly dismounted and bandaged up Sandy's nose with his handkerchief! The bullet had made a nice clean hole and did not appear to have hurt the pony in the least.

It was the only casualty suffered by the counter-attackers, before whose onslaught the Germans had fled precipitately downhill. Elsewhere along the ridge the enemy thrusting forward had also met a resistance more stubborn than he had reason to expect, and seemed to be satisfied to repeat the tactics he had already found to pay him so handsomely. Yet had the Germans made one determined onslaught then they must have overrun us completely. Instead they tarried, and their inaction was once more our opportunity to organise a defence. Even with the Wiltshires the line could only be made to stretch a short distance, and its flanks were in the air, for the French had vanished. Moreover, both officers and men of Grogan's force were so exhausted that they would never have stood up under any further immediate pressure, most of them having reached the state when not even the imminence of personal danger could keep them awake or make them stir their tired limbs. Poor Thompson, for example, had managed to reach the Bouleuse ridge in the flight from Treslon, had sat himself down for a moment to regain his breath, and even while the Germans were making their attempt to carry the position, had fallen asleep. Such efforts as we could spare to wake him had no effect, and asleep he lay until conditions had quietened down, when he was lifted on to a charger by one of the grooms and borne from the scene of strife, still asleep !

The Brigadier remained a marvel of endurance, and this was well since just before dusk there arrived some more welcome reinforcements in the shape of two composite units, made up of all sorts of infantrymen, gunners, transport men, officers' servants, and drummers, chiefly of the 8th Division, and numbering about seven hundred in all.

The coming of dusk accordingly found the defenders strengthened but the situation critical. The Bouleuse position was not a good one, as the field of fire was limited and the Germans were established in considerable strength in the thickets not three hundred yards below.

Then the glad news came that we were to be relieved.

The signallers had carried their telephone back to a copse on the reverse slopes of the ridge, and gave us the message from 8th Division that the 19th Division were taking over the command of the front. The G.O.C. 56th Infantry Brigade would take over from Grogan the command of all the troops on the Bouleuse ridge—this was in effect the divisional front !

Sitting with the signallers was Prance's servant, a Scot, although serving in his officer's regiment, the South Wales Borderers. He, poor chap, was very, very maudlin. The shock of Prance's death and the effect of much good champagne on an empty stomach had been too much for him. Him we had to leave with his tears, as when night fell, orders came for the Brigadier, now in a state bordering on collapse, to return to Divisional Headquarters. When he went he took Ledward, Thompson and me with him.

THE MARNE

VI

THE MARNE

THIS relief marks the end of the part officially played in the battle by the 8th Division and also the 23rd Brigade. The emphasis must be on the word " officially " for, as so frequently happened, there was a wide discrepancy between the terms of the order and the way these were interpreted. It was a relief of staffs only, a change-over in command. During the night of May 29–30 the 8th Division handed over the front to the 19th Division and on the next morning retired comfortably across the Marne to Villers-au-Bois. The 23rd Brigade likewise handed over to 56th Brigade, and this may have affected the troops in line, for Grogan was irreplaceable. Otherwise neither the change of command nor the arrival of the fresh troops of the 19th Division made any difference to the gallant band of survivors of the 8th, 25th, and 50th Divisions on the Bouleuse ridge. These remnants were not relieved, though their less sorely tried fellows of the 21st Division were withdrawn that night.

The 19th Division—whose sign was somewhat fancifully, perhaps, a butterfly—had been rushed up so quickly that its transport had been unable to keep pace, and arrangements had accordingly been made that we should help them out with rations and ammunition until their own supplies could arrive. Our A.A. and Q.M.G., Lord Feilding, short, red-faced, and black-moustached, asked me if I would like another job, and this was how it was that, after three or four hours' sleep snatched in a deserted cottage, I found myself at dawn on the 30th in charge of all the limbers of the Division which were in the forward area. It was not an imposing command as there were only about twenty-five of them, but it was an independent one. My orders were to report to the 56th Brigade, and then, as a further withdrawal was obviously impending, to make my way rearwards, laying, as I went, dumps of rations and S.A.A. at places to be arranged with the Brigade.

My first call on rising was at their Headquarters, which were in a house on the outskirts of Sarcy. The Brigadier and two of his staff had just come down to breakfast and, after our experiences of the past three days, it was a surprise to see a table properly laid out with tea and bread and marmalade. I had not broken my fast, but the officers appeared so concerned that their usual eggs and bacon were not forthcoming that they omitted to offer me any refreshment. Nor was their attitude particularly congenial, although I realise that against their neat uniforms and polished belts and buttons I must have looked dirty, ragged, and unsoldierly, and no very agreeable decoration for a breakfast-room. At the time I was furious ; furious because I was hungry ; furious because they should presume to have a breakfast-room ; and furious to think that those who were to take over our responsibilities should be so out of touch with reality as to complain because a hot meal was not punctual. I was as polite as discipline demanded, and no more. After all, they were new to the open warfare game of hare and hounds, with the enemy in the latter and more agreeable part, and I left them, saying to myself, " You wait ! You'll get your eyes opened !" Nor had they to wait long.

I returned to my limbers which were lined up in Sarcy, and as I was making a sustaining but unappetising breakfast off a cold Maconochie, one of the grooms produced Peggy—Peggy, none the worse for her experiences of the day before, the same docile but stubborn creature that I knew so well. Had I not rescued her a year before from a gunteam because she was so well mannered, giving in exchange a nasty brute whose antics were too much for me and would be well checked in harness ! About 9 a.m. a message came from 56th Brigade that the enemy had taken Lhery on the left and was also making progress on the right. This was alarming. I had kept the transport in Sarcy because from just outside it there were two avenues of retreat open to me, one going left of a central ridge of hills to Ville-en-Tardenois, and the other on the right to Chaumuzy. Now both were threatened, and it was a toss-up which to take. I decided on the latter because it seemed more direct and because 8th Division were to have left an advanced headquarters in Chaumuzy. We departed at once, and at the gallop, but even so came under fire both from guns and infantry patrols as soon as we were outside the village. Luckily the road was clear and we were moving fast, and the only damage we sustained was that Mathews, the transport officer of the 2nd

Middlesex, got a "cushy" wound in the hand, the sort of "blighty one" that old soldiers dreamed about.

We had not finished congratulating ourselves on this escape when we ran into more trouble, two-way traffic congestion of the worst kind ; and joined a stream of English and French wagons, cookers, and mule-teams which was struggling to make its way through an oncoming flood of transport, guns and men of both nationalities, striving desperately to reach the firing-line. Once more we experienced the hopeless agony of crawling along in dust and sweat, with the knowledge that the enemy we had just eluded was coming on fast behind us.

Frequently we could only progress a few hundred paces at a time, then halt for some minutes and on again, yet for all its stumbling monotony, the march was not without incident. At one halt a batch of German prisoners, under the escort of two French cavalrymen, shambled past us on the roadside. As soon as they came abreast of a smock-clad peasant who was sitting close to us, he jumped to his feet, seized two stout sticks and, pressing one on an English soldier, motioned him to follow. He then rushed in among the defence-less Germans, lashing out on them with all his strength, the escort merely grinning at what they appeared to find a very good joke. Needless to say, this berserk example was not followed by the English-man, who, like the rest of us, must have felt a little ashamed to see defenceless prisoners so maltreated.

Another incident was equally disturbing and illustrated very clearly the feelings of the inhabitants towards us. As we passed some old peasants who showed no signs of leaving their holding to join the retreat, one of our men good-naturedly shouted to them in pidgin-French that the enemy would soon be on them : " Allemand venez vite. Beaucoup bombarde ! " They replied angrily that they were staying where they were, that they had experienced the Germans in 1914—some of them claimed even to remember 1870 — and would stay with them again. " The Germans anyway were better than the British ! " they declared, and rushing to the roadside, they spat at us in their rage. They were observed by a French officer, one of the very few incidentally that I saw that day, who was gentleman enough to blush for his countrymen. " Ne t'en fais pas ! " he said, coming across to me, " They did the same to us at Verdun ! " It was a bitter commentary on the Gallic spirit in defeat. The observations of our men were equally bitter. At this period the conviction was growing among the rank and file that " we were fighting on the wrong side," a conviction I had heard expressed many times since 1917, but never before with such feeling.

All morning we plodded on, buoyed up with the vague hope that at Chaumuzy things would be all right. There we should get some explicit orders as to what to do and where to make for, a rest from this interminable slow march and something to eat and drink. It was the hottest hour of the day when we pulled up on the outskirts of the village, and I went on on foot to find the advanced headquarters office.

It was an ugly scene that met me. Chaos was

king.   The narrow, cobbled streets were blocked
from end to end with transport and guns ; with
farm carts piled high with chairs, mattresses, fodder,
fowls in crates, and all the pathetic impedimenta
of the peasant refugee ; and with drunken French
infantry, both whites and coloured men.   They
had apparently looted the wineshops and a big
canteen and, demoralised as they were drunken,
were in a state bordering on hysteria.   All semblance
of discipline had gone.   They were as liable to laugh
as to weep, to fight as to run, and their shouts and
wild laughter mingled with bangs as rifles and
pistols went off, whether by accident or design.
It was the first and only time in the war that I
witnessed a real collapse of morale, and it was a
terrifying spectacle.   As unobtrusively as I could,
so as to avoid any unpleasantness, I searched about
for the divisional office, and eventually found an
English straggler who told me that " the staff
officers had gone an hour or so before."   There was
therefore nothing to do but push on somehow,
and at all costs to get clear of Chaumuzy at once,
which as an important road junction was bound
to be shelled as soon as the enemy got within range ;
and when it was, was certain to be a death-trap.
Somehow we did get clear, sneaking our way
through, one or two vehicles at a time, and careful
not to precipitate any clashes with the French, but
we were very fortunate, and were indeed still
clattering over the cobbles on the main Épernay
road when a heavy gun began firing on the village.
In the street we had just left the first shell struck a
petrol lorry.   With a roar and a flash, the hot
breath of which beat on our necks, it exploded,

making a fearful crematory pyre of the men and horses around.

This was enough. I decided to shake off the shackles of congestion, and risk a cut across country, hoping by making a detour to regain the Épernay road ahead of the traffic block. I wheeled the limbers, most of which were now empty, into the fields on the right and gave them orders to pick their way so as to rejoin the road between Marfaux and Pourcy. As soon as they were started I left them and cantered on ahead in an effort to find some responsible staff officer who could tell me where we were to make for ; whether we should search for a refilling point and load up again, or move right back to the remainder of the divisional transport. I did not go alone, for I had by this time somehow attached to myself a lance-corporal of the 1st Worcesters, whom I had mounted on a spare charger and who now acted as my groom, my valet, and, when opportunity offered, my cook. His post was a sinecure while it lasted, though for the last-named duty he carried a large salvaged iron kettle slung from his saddle.

We rode at first through the rich grass of water-meadows beside a limpid stream, then on the shorter grass of chalky uplands, and on hard-rutted farm tracks. It was a restful countryside, and the war seemed to have been left behind on the roads. The quietude and the warm sunshine combined with our lack of sleep to make us drowsy, so that it needed a conscious effort to prevent ourselves dozing off in the saddle. Over the brow of a hillock we went, a hillock which dropped sharply down a hawthorn-covered slope. A shrill squeal, followed by a high-pitched neighing challenge roused me to wakefulness. There to my right, in the cover of the hawthorns, was drawn up a squadron of dark-blue cloaked "chasseurs d'Afrique," each man sitting an Arab stallion. And I was riding Peggy ! It was a reminder that there were other dangers than bullets, and, kicking the mare into a gallop, I made off as fast as possible.

When at last we struck the road again we saw with relief that, except for a few French lorries whirling along in their enveloping dust-shrouds, it was free of traffic, but though this would be an advantage to my limbers it was of no immediate help to me in my quest for our Staff. We jogged along, the sun was very hot and the desire for sleep was very strong. Blast ! Something slashed me smartly across the face. Automatically I pulled Peggy up : found that she had wandered off the road into a pinewood, and that I had been fast asleep. A branch striking me on the face had wakened me.

It should by then have been tea-time, but I had not much farther to go. At a road junction one of the lorries, driven at a more than usually ferocious pace, swung round on two wheels into the left-hand fork so close in front of Peggy's nose that she was forced backwards into the ditch, where she toppled over, decanting me into a field. I yelled a curse at the driver for his carelessness, but was surprised to find the imperturbable Peggy none the worse. Then, blessed sight, I descried Ramsbotham, our D.A.A.G., riding towards me.

Herwald Ramsbotham was a soldier by necessity. By choice of profession he was an advocate, who

had been called to the bar after a distinguished
Oxford career, yet the curious thing was that with
his trim moustache, his monocle, and one eyebrow
cocked with an air of quizzical inquiry he looked
very much the type of regular soldier. His monocle
was attached to his person by a cord, but this always
seemed to me a superfluous precaution, for nothing
could disturb that eye-piece. One of my more
cherished war memories is of Ramsbotham making
one of his infrequent appearances in my divisional
officers' soccer XI. It was a raw day and we were
about to play the 2nd Rifle Brigade. While we
were kicking in at goal, Ramsbotham had kept on
his British warm over his football kit, on his head
his uniform cap, and in his eye the monocle. He
had turned to talk to some one on the touchline
when a random punt from the goalkeeper propelled
the wet ball smack on to his head. Away flew the
cap, but the monocle remained in place !

So now, dust-stained and unshaven as he was, his
monocle was a valuable link with more ordered
times, something almost symbolic of another age.
It was for me a most welcome proof that I was in
touch again with order and discipline, and with
my own people, although for the moment all
Ramsbotham could tell me definitely was that
Colonel Feilding and one or two others were in
Nanteuil la Fosse, a few miles farther back, where
the 19th Division had set up their headquarters. He
advised me to leave my Worcester groom behind
to guide the limbers there when they should show
up and, this done, I rode on with him, giving him
as we went an account of our stewardship such as
it had been.

I heard that Feilding had had a nasty experience in Chaumuzy that morning. He was on his horse superintending the passage of some of our men and wagons when a drunken Frenchman had rushed up to him and without warning levelled a revolver at him, yelling that he was going to shoot. Feilding sat quite still, looked the half-crazy " poilu " full in the eyes, and, with the curl of his lip which I knew so well, said contemptuously, " Allez, sale soldat noir ! " The insult and the tone of quiet authority in which it was uttered sunk into the fuddled brain. The man lowered his weapon and moved almost shamefacedly away. It was one of those assertions of personality in the face of danger which abound in " strong man " literature, but are less frequently authenticated in real life.

I had had many opportunities of seeing Feilding at close quarters during the alarms and excursions of the preceding months, and I never saw him rattled.

There was the morning of March 22 at Harbonnières, when with the Division thrown in to help stem the breach on the Somme, he had stood, legs apart, as calmly as if before his own fireplace, giving orders and instructions to the great tidal wave of humanity that roared past him from the threatened land in front. There were military drivers of tractors, steam-rollers and ploughs, ambulances and wagons. There were red-cross sisters and railway-men. There were labour troops of all nationalities, Italians, Chinese, West Indians, and British ; and they had none of them any more connection with the 8th Division than Feilding had with them. Yet, seeing him they appealed to him instinctively to tell them where to go or what to do, and he as naturally told them to the best of his ability.

There was the dawn of April 1 at Jumel when after days without proper rest and a night of constant effort in driving rain, he had said to me, " I'm going to have a couple of hours' sleep now," and lying down in his greatcoat underneath the table in a brick-floored cottage kitchen the door of which opened on to the main road, he had fallen at once to sleep, waking as he had said about two hours later, ready once more for action.

No matter how tense or disagreeable the situation he always seemed to be planted firmly on his short legs, and his smile only varied in degree whether he was angry or pleased.

So now when I met him at Nanteuil la Fosse his answers to my questions came readily and unequivocally. The limbers would not refill. They would bivouac near the village that night and next morning I should take them off and see them safely across the Marne. It was probably a case of counting my chickens, because I had no guarantee that they would ever arrive; and I was almost as surprised as I was relieved to greet them about 7 p.m. after an entirely uneventful cross-country journey which had brought them on to the Épernay road close to Pourcy.

The 19th Division having occupied all the houses in the village, the few officers of 8th Division who had been left in the forward area for liaison and to see that any odd remnants of the Division other than fighting men were evacuated, had been unable to find rooms for themselves either to eat in or sleep in. All that remained to them was a com-

modious brick cellar, underneath one of the larger
houses, and used by its rightful owner for the
storage of his potatoes, a large heap of which,
already whiskery with white shoots, was piled up
against the side. Thither we repaired at sundown,
Feilding, Ramsbotham, Wallace—Brigade-major of
24th Brigade—and myself, for some much-needed
refreshment for body and mind. Never before
can those aged brick walls have regarded a more
comical spectacle than the supper which was served
there that night. We were all ravenous, but as
will readily be understood, food, after the flight of
many of the civilians and the passage of French
troops, accustomed by tradition and necessity to
live on the country, was difficult to beg, buy, or
steal. For all that, Reddington, Feilding's Cold-
streamer servant, had procured a loaf or two of
bread, a tin of sardines, some jam (ration, English),
and some bottles of white wine. It should here
be interpolated that wine was, not unnaturally, the
one comestible that was available in quantity and
quality, for were we not now fighting almost among
the vineyards of the famous Champagne firms, and
it was entertaining to see Mr. Atkins, dust-white
and unshaven, sitting by the edge of a road knocking
the top off a bottle of Moët et Chandon's best to
wash down his stale bread and his bully beef !
To revert, Reddington had contrived a dining-table
out of an old trestle and boxes, whereon he had laid
out his meagre viands with all the array he could
manage. He then announced to the Colonel,
" Supper is ready, m'lord," as if we were in Gros-
venor Square, instead of a potato-cellar in an obscure
village in France.

We fell to with a will, until everything except a few crumbs had disappeared and the wine bottles were emptied, and afterwards sank ourselves in a sleep of sheer exhaustion on the couch provided by the heap of potatoes. Wallace and I rolled up together in an old piece of sacking, but during the night we parted company. Morning found Wallace still on the potatoes, minus the sacking, and I had the coverlet but had rolled off without the least disturbance to my slumbers on to the stone floor.

I did not want for evidence that the night had been as cold as my couch hard, and it was a very stiff and muscle-cramped officer who climbed into the saddle to lead the column of limbers on the last stage of their journey rearwards. It was a pleasant ride, as the road I took passed the fringe of the Forêt de la Montagne de Reims, and then going by Romery, dropped down the steep slopes to the wide-flowing Marne at Damery. Beside the stone structure rose an unfinished pontoon bridge. All through the four years of the war, British engineers had diligently carted their pontoons about with them, and even three years of position warfare, when there was no likelihood of anything wider than a trench to be crossed, had not persuaded the authorities to discard them for some articles of more practical value. No, the pontoons must be kept as part of a field company's equipment. One never knew. Now there was a wide river where an emergency crossing might be necessary, but, sad to relate, the pontoons were found to be no longer water-tight !

From Damery we made for the Bois de Boursault, in the forest of Enghien, where all that was left of the divisional transport, first and second line, was concentrated. Here I took leave of my Worcester lance-corporal, sending him to report to his regimental quartermaster, and, handing over my command, made my way to the huts where the remains of 23rd Brigade Headquarters had regathered.

There I found the Brigadier and Ledward, Thompson and Parsloe, and a relief Brigade-major; and more of the other ranks than I had expected to see again. They were a mournful party and there was no one with enough energy of spirit to rouse them from their dejection. The Brigadier was particularly dispirited and irritable, which was understandable, suffering as he was from nervous exhaustion after his great effort, as well as from a sense of loss at the destruction of his command, and, more personally, the death of Prance. In the gloom of the twilight he took me with him round the three regimental transports, in an attempt to glean some definite information as to the extent of our losses, for official reports as well as for our own satisfaction. This was a tragic task in itself, and more tragic still in the detail it disclosed. The best that could be said about the fate of most of our friends was that they were missing. Messages reached us that the Germans were still forging ahead, and, most alarming, that they had reached the Marne at Château Thierry. For all we knew they might already be across it. Meanwhile there was not a murmur about our being relieved, and if our poor services were still essential the outlook must be hopeless indeed. In short, and taking everything into consideration, those who went to bed that night feeling that all was lost, might have been excused. Possibly because I had not had so trying an experience or because my spirits were naturally more buoyant, or both, I remained determined to see the bright side, and confidently predicted, without any reason, that everything would be " all right."

As stragglers had dribbled back during the course of the action, they had been gathered up with as much diligence as raindrops in a thirsty land, and on the morrow, June 2, a final muster was made of these, and a drastic comb-out of all transport men, bandsmen, stretcher-bearers, officers' servants, and others not needed for essential duties. The result was a grand total of 500 men of all arms of the Division, who were banded together and sent up that evening to join the 750 other survivors who had been gathered together in the firing-line which now ran through the Bois de Courton. The whole force was then split into two composite battalions, the commands of which were given to the only two lieutenant-colonels left—E. M. Beale of the Machine Gun Corps and D. Mitchell of the 22nd Durham Light Infantry (Pioneers).

Simultaneously it was agreed that the likelihood of the Germans crossing the Marne farther east was a threat to our concentration in the Bois de Boursault, and we were ordered to move. All the heavy wagons and general impedimenta were to be sent to the rear, but in order to look after our own men, the first line transport was again to be left in the forward area and take over the duty of rationing the two composite battalions.

One day had been enough to convince me that

existence behind the line was as depressing as it was inactive. I had tasted also the sweets of independent command, and thirsted for more, so I went and begged Feilding to let me again take charge of the forward transport. To my great joy he said " Yes," and I at once made myself scarce before the arrangements might be changed or some one else with higher qualifications appointed to the job. My orders were to keep the transport at a place called La Loge Turbanne, where two roads forked about half a mile outside the hamlet of Pierry, and some three miles south-west of Épernay ; and which had been chosen because from it a choice of routes lay open to us, one eastwards to Châlons, the other southwards. Here the supply-lorries would deliver rations to me in bulk as they received them from railhead, and it was to be my responsibility to parcel them out and carry them forward to the quartermaster of the composite battalions.

Not unnaturally, after such intensive practice, we at first went about our work with our loins girded for further flight, and were kept very much on the alert by disturbing rumours of enemy successes near Château Thierry. But one day passed, then another, then a third, and almost insensibly we grew aware that the front had become stationary. We realised that we were now well on the flank of the deep narrow salient made by the German break-through, and although violent fighting was still in progress at its apex, on our sector there was a lull which was to endure as long as we remained in the Champagne. For ten days our composite battalions hung on to their positions, but except for two local attacks against the Montagne de Bligny on June 6, the enemy made no further attempt to advance against us. His offensive had spent itself ; to use a motoring metaphor, it had over-run its engine. Not until July did the Germans make their last large-scale, despairing effort to enlarge their salient, and drive through to Paris ; and so invite Pétain's dramatic counter-attack against their eastern flank, which was to drive them back almost to the very trenches which they had left to attack us at dawn on May 27.

Quickly the front settled down, trenches were dug, and the familiar uneventful routine of position warfare re-established.

As quickly we all dropped into our several routines. Although it had long since ceased to represent a fighting unit, 8th Divisional Head-quarters remained at Villers-au-Bois. Its surviving fighting men reverted to trench life in a new and decorative setting against a back-cloth of immense woods, and at La Loge Turbanne we lived a life of alfresco luxury and ease. During these last days we were rather like a rowing eight which had eased up and was resting on its oars after a long and gruelling row, though with the knowledge, that dead beat as we were, we might at any moment have to be off at another racing-start.

Although La Loge Turbanne was within the area of hostilities, it seemed to have survived from another world. It was for France a large farmstead, a square white house with extensive out-buildings clustered round a cobbled yard ; in the middle the inevitable midden. Facing it, across the road was a wide stretch of meadow-land with a Dutch barn full of hay, and a pleasant stream twinkling over its gravelled bed. The weather was glorious.

What more could even an August holiday camper have desired ? We had fallen into Paradise. For our sleeping quarters we had the choice of the close animal-scented warmth of the lofts above the cow-byres, or the cool fragrance of the hay-stacks, open to the air, but under a protecting roof. Most of us preferred the out-of-doors, and at night the stack must have looked like an ant-heap, so full was it of human beings. For our morning wash, for our cooking and for watering our horses, there was the rivulet, clear, clean, and cold. For our sustenance we had army rations in plenty, the farm folk could spare us limited quantities of eggs and milk ; and in Épernay, the city of champagne, merchants were selling off at panic prices, for already their shops and "caves" were under fire and no one could tell when the Germans might force an entry. The sudden change from emergency rations to a rich and plentiful diet, together with the not very arduous daily task of riding up to the Bois de Courton and back, transformed haggard scarecrows into healthy specimens in a few days, and it is not difficult to understand that many of the men were very loath to leave the farm when orders finally came for us to do so. It was also a novel experience for the P.B.I. to do supply work, and some of the secrets of the A.S.C.—notably why ration beef or mutton never possessed kidneys, at least never when it reached the troops for whom it was destined— were disclosed. Otherwise I had " nothing to report."

One morning a message came from Grogan

asking me to go into Épernay and procure for him
some white wine, still wine as a change from the
" fizzy " product which we soon learned was a luxury
which very quickly cloys. I found the streets silent
and deserted, the shops shut and shuttered, bricks,
leaves, and fine dust strewing the cobble sets—all
the well-known symptoms of a bombarded town.
At intervals there came the slow moan of an approaching shell, rising to an exultant yell as it fell to its
target, the rending crash as it burst, tossing bricks
and splinters into the air in a cloud of red dust.
I had not chosen the best time to go bargain-
hunting ! The only human being in sight was a
figure in faded horizon-blue and steel helmet,
leaning nonchalantly, hands in breeches pockets,
against a window-sill. To him I addressed myself
in my best French, asking could he tell me of any
" marchand de vin " who was open to do business.
He let me make my little speech, and then his face,
covered in grey stubble, slowly broke into a smile,
and he answered me in the sing-song accents of
East Anglia. He was a Cambridgeshire man, he
told me, and had been employed in the racing
stables near Paris. As he had been earning French
wages, he had been caught up into the French
Army on mobilisation, and there he had remained,
in spite of his efforts to transfer to his own folks,
a " poilu " at five sous the day.

The only section of the Division for whom there
was no relaxation of effort was the R.A.M.C. On
the contrary while we were lazing in the sunshine,
and the composite battalions alternating spells of
sentry-duty with sleep in the line, the doctors were
slaving day and night at higher pressure than ever.

With one exception, which only emphasises the record, every medical officer attached to the infantry was either killed, wounded, or missing before the battle had lasted three days. One of the field ambulances had been captured intact. Even the A.D.M.S. had been wounded. Meanwhile an ebb-tide of wounded, a slow-moving flood of men in stained white bandages, dusty khaki, and faded blue, was tumbling into the French casualty clearing stations in a volume with which the French medical services could never have coped even had they been intact. They had neither the staff, resources, nor organisation to evacuate the wretched men, much less to give them proper surgical treatment, and even had they been in a position to do this it would naturally have been a case of Frenchmen first. Moreover, we were execrated as " Sales Anglais." Here was a vital problem which was tackled resolutely by Bourdillon who, here, there, and everywhere as he had been during the retreat from the Aisne, now mobilised the remaining doctors and after detailing two for duty with the battalions in line, took the others off to the big French C.C.S. in Épernay. Far from being welcomed, they were uncivilly allowed to help, and there for days they acted as dressers, physicians, and surgeons, and sweated as nurses, stretcher-bearers, and orderlies, until practically all the British wounded had been evacuated by ambulance, or on the hospital trains on which the French grudged any Englishman a passage. How many lives this devoted band saved will never be known. It is certainly considerable, and in itself the only reward that they will receive. It is also possibly the one they would most prize.

The removal of some of Seeley's Canadian cavalrymen from a schoolroom on the Somme which was being used as a French casualty station in March, had given me a good idea of the great gulf fixed between French and British methods of treating casualties, and a dressing-station we took over near Romery provided me with a reminder that made me thank Heaven I was fighting under British command. It also helped me to understand why the mortality among the French was so high. It was a long, wooden hut, black and gloomy, its windows cobwebbed, fly-bespattered and tight shut, its dry mud floor ankle-deep in blood-soaked, fœtid straw, on which the wounded men were lying. One dresser, white-faced and harassed, a mere lad, who had still to complete his medical studies at the Sorbonne, was struggling mightily to attend them all at the same time, leaving one as another cried out ; without the requisite knowledge, without experience, instruments, antiseptics or disinfectants, without even adequate food or drink for aching bellies or mouths parched by fever. Quite by chance I saw the same hut a few hours afterwards. The straw had disappeared, the stamped floor shone with brushing, the sharp smell of antiseptics and the opened windows had ousted the rank decaying odour ; and those sufferers who had not been evacuated were lying on stretchers covered with a blanket, two orderlies under the direction of an M.O. washing and dressing their wounds. The contrast was so striking that it might have been designed to illustrate the pro-gress of medical hygiene from 1870 to the present day !

The part played by Bourdillon's team of doctors
was not, of course, known to us at the time. Indeed
all thoughts of wounds, bandages, and operating-
tables had temporarily receded into the subconscious,
and with that absolute acceptance of the present
which during those years was at once our characteristic and our defence, we had sunk completely
into our surroundings, so that when the once
eagerly desired orders for our withdrawal reached
us, they were no longer a matter for jubilation.
The 8th Division would leave the area of the French
Armies on June 14, the orders informed us. For
me they meant parting with the many good friends
among transport drivers, brakesmen, and dispatch
riders, who now dispersed to rejoin their units
preparatory to entraining ; and also a return once
more to my subordinate position at 23rd Brigade
Headquarters at Vertus. But only for one night,
as the last job that Feilding put on me was a watch-
ing-brief over the entraining arrangements of the
Brigade. For one more day therefore I was an
independent unit, and the last picture that remains
in my mind of the Champagne in war-time, like the
first, centres in a railway station.

Three stations were scheduled for the Division—
Sommesous, Sezanne, and Fère Champenoise—all
three of which lay to the south in the " Champagne
Pouilleuse," as distinct from the rich, wine-growing
northern territory we had traversed since May 27.
It was a bleak, sand-buried, barren country, a
country of wide hawthorn brakes and marshland,
a country of no colour and few features, where
apparently little grew except the scattered crosses,
souvenirs of Autumn 1914, on which fluttered

ragged tricolour rosettes, and dull tinsel flowers—
" Morts au champ d'honneur."

I was overseer at Sommesous, which was little
more than a wayside halt, with weeds luxuriating
between the metals which shimmered in the heat.
Its equipment, particularly the signals, its platform-
lessness, and its generally unkempt appearance,
proclaimed unmistakably to the eye its alien identity,
but the smells of a railway station vary little the
world over, so that my nose carried me back to any
English country station under a summer sun.
There was the same warm medley of smells—the
grass-scented breath of the fields, the tarry smell of
the sleepers, and the occasional whiff of locomotive
smoke mingling with the animal smells, of horse-
dung, sweat-soaked leather harness, and the heated
bodies of horse, mule, and man, as the loading went
on. All day the long, shabby trains of grey vans
and flat trucks shuffled into the station and out
again with much jerking and creaking as if in
protest at their loads. Men coaxed and compelled
the animals to entrain, and heaved and strained to
pull wagons on to the trucks and lash them securely.
I had nothing to do but look on, a drowsy job in the
sunshine, and I found myself automatically reading
off the inscription on the railway-vans and wonder-
ing why it sounded so odd—at one end the word
" Étiquettes," at the other " Hommes 40. Chevaux
en long 8." In some curious way it seemed to
suggest an apology for the behaviour of the cargo !

If graphic proof of the Division's obliteration
were needed, here it was. Normally an infantry
battalion required a whole train to accommodate it
and its transport. Now the 2nd Middlesex shared

the same train as 23rd Brigade Headquarters, the
23rd Trench Mortar Battery, and the Signal
Section, with their respective transports—and then
there was ample room for all ! The 2nd Devons
shared another with the 26th Field Ambulance.

It was an entrainment of Quartermasters' Stores
(a mere term now to describe a few men most of
whose stores had long since become German
property !) ; the remains of the transport vehicles
and horses, and a scattering of troops, the bulk of
whom had arrived as reinforcement details during
the last three or four days.

If I wished to indulge the years-after-the-event
imagination so prevalent among war-writers, I
should write that it was an entrainment of ghosts.
This would sound well, but it would be nonsense.
It was a cheerful occasion, on the contrary, a
rendezvous, and as we met we joked and laughed,
in the knowledge that we were off, this time certainly for a period of rest and refitting behind the
line. Many people whom I might have expected to
see were missing, of course, but there were others I
was glad to meet, and present company during the
war was always more important than absent friends.
That was the unconscious result of the philosophy
which made life bearable.

Among the many survivors who entrained that
day was one I was particularly, though admittedly
sentimentally, glad to see. As the skeleton remains
of the luckless, gallant 5th Battery drove into the
station yard, Mickey O'Sullivan, their veterinary
officer, brought with him old " Dublin." " Dublin"
was a character. He was a cat, large, black, and
plebeian, and what he did not know about trench

warfare was not worth knowing. Could he not tell which way a shell was coming, and to watch him was to have a shrewd idea of whether it was likely to burst close or not. If he did not move there was no need to worry. " Dublin " went right through the war, landing in France with the 8th Division on November 5, 1914, and leaving after the Armistice. He returned to die of old age many years afterwards in his native Ireland.

When the last wagon was lashed on to the last train, and the last officer stepped aboard, and when with much penny-trumpet blowing and escaping of steam, it had pulled out of the station, I meta-phorically kissed my hand to the Champagne ; and followed in the comparative luxury of a Wolseley motor ambulance, bearing away with me another full pack, crammed this time with the wine of the country at 5d. the bottle !

THE RECKONING

VII

THE RECKONING

Of all the battles on the Western Front, that of the Aisne and the Marne, 1918, was at once the most remarkable and the most disastrous to British arms.

It was the enemy's last great offensive, the most brilliant and the most successful, not only better planned than his others, but the secret of his preparations better kept. The first break-through was so overwhelming, so complete, that nothing he did before or after could be compared to it. His artillery preparation was of a violence and accuracy that in the opinion of the most seasoned soldiers far outdid any other barrage they were under. Moreover, he wasted no gunfire on our front line positions. These he flattened by trench-mortars, reserving his artillery for the battle zone and strategic points farther back. His aircraft quickly drove the few French planes out of the sky, and throughout the battle we had no air support. Moreover, he brought up tanks both against the 25th Brigade in the initial assault and in order to break down the remains of resistance on our own Brigade front. These were converted British machines, and luckily for us, do not seem to have been seen after the first morning. Indeed many of them found the width of our trenches an insuperable obstacle.

Notwithstanding the thoroughness of his organisation and the energy and enterprise with which he exploited his success, the enemy was considerably helped, first, in the field of strategy by the failure of the French Command to appreciate the situation ; and secondly by the tactical weakness of the defence.

I have already emphasised the fatal obstinacy of the French Army Commander in shutting his eyes to the lessons that should have been learnt from the two earlier German offensives, and particularly the importance of defence in depth.   If, for example, we had on May 26 withdrawn from our front trenches all but a few observers ; had stationed garrisons plentifully supplied with machine-guns in strong points such as the Bois des Buttes and Bois de Gernicourt ; if we had, as was recommended, pulled our guns out of their well-registered positions and stationed them even in the open south of the Aisne, the story of the enemy's advance might have been very different. The Germans' tremendous barrage would have blown itself out on empty trenches and emplacements, and our artillery would have been in a position to rake the attackers as they approached the obstacles of the rivers.   Had they then succeeded in crossing these, we should have had intact the main body of our infantry and been able to fall back on the highly organised systems of defence which the French had prepared in rear, and all of which had successively to be abandoned, most of them without ever having been occupied.   But as I have indicated, French Army Headquarters appeared to be still imbued with the idea that " l'audace " could overcome artillery, and adhered to dispositions which were out of date at Port

Arthur. Perhaps the fact that the British had suggested an alternative method had something to do with this stubbornness, for when the Germans next attacked, the French dispositions in depth before Rheims remain a model of this type of defence. The French showed they could learn quickly enough when they wished. Equally, unless it was the Supreme Command's definite intention to let troops as tired as we were act as the buffer to take the shock of the first German onslaught, which is unthinkable, the French intelligence service was also sadly at fault. The French certainly knew that the Germans had made preparations for an attack and had built field fortifications to meet the blow when it came. They had ample and sufficient warning that it was coming and where, and even the grace of twenty-four hours' certain knowledge before it came, yet they did nothing. It is a sobering reflection that the first act of the unified command on the Western Front was to send battle-shattered British divisions down to rest on the precise sector which barred the road to Paris, and which the enemy had chosen for his next offensive !

Secondly, the Germans were helped by the tactical weakness of the defence. To begin with, our men were tired. They were also too few. Battalions much under strength were each made responsible for holding about one thousand yards of front, so that there were great gaps in the trenches without a sentry-post. The troops had barely time to know their whereabouts or where the trenches led. The support battalions were accommodated in tunnel dug-outs in which they lost their way, and many of them were killed or taken by the enemy as they emerged.   It may be that with more experience of the sector a more coherent defence might have been organised, but it is very doubtful in the circumstances if anything that was done would have had much effect, especially in view of the collapse of all artillery and air support and the positions we were ordered to take up.

The Higher Command literally asked for trouble and they got it.   This is possibly inaccurate : *we* got it.

The foregoing must not be held to detract from the skill with which the Germans took advantage of their opportunity.   I have already remarked on the amazing speed at which they came on.   In the four days, May 27–30, they advanced and we fought, walked, and ran twenty-eight miles !   At Château Thierry they were only thirty-five miles from Paris.   It was a crowning mercy that they had no cavalry.   How many times during the retreat did we thank Heaven for this !   The sight of a few mounted men in the distance would at once start a ripple of anxiety, the word " Cavalry ! " being whispered and passed from mouth to mouth down the firing-line.   Men looked apprehensively over their shoulders, fearful lest horsemen might be already behind them.   Cavalry was the one factor which would have smashed the morale of the defence in a twinkling.

Almost more remarkable than the rapidity of their pursuit was the speed with which they advanced over the trench system itself.   Millis relates that when, during the flight of Brigade Headquarters from the dug-outs to Pontavert, the thick mist lifted for a second, it showed German infantrymen actually moving forward parallel with the Brigade party !   A subaltern of the Devon Regiment, who was captured, told me that he was in a shell-hole with a few men firing hard at enemy skirmishers advancing across the open near the Bois des Buttes, between him and which ran a road protected by a large camouflage screen.   The battle was still hot. Then a chance shell wrecked the screen, to reveal a German infantry battalion marching in column of fours down the road.

The complete disintegration of formations and the impossibility, owing to road congestion and the rapidity of the retreat, of the higher staff keeping in close touch with the situation, resulted in a " soldiers' battle."   Time after time the situation was only saved by the gallantry and resource of some officer or man whose deeds have gone unheard-of and unrecognised.   History will never know the details of the deadly isolated struggles which must have been fought out in the mists and marshes of the Aisne, in the valleys of the Vesle and Ardre, amid the standing corn on the successive ridges or in the vast woods of the Montagnes de Reims. Time and the evidence of chance eye-witnesses have lifted the curtain sufficiently to allow us a glimpse here and there.   One such glimpse reveals the stand of the 2nd Devons in front of Pontavert. Those of the Battalion who had not been taken or killed on coming out of their tunnels had fallen back, fighting at every step, almost to the bridge, by which time they were surrounded.   Here in the last trench north of the river they were seen by an artillery officer holding " a position in which they were entirely without hope of help, but were fighting on grimly.   The commanding officer (Lieut.-Colonel R. H. Anderson-Morshead) himself was calmly writing his orders with a perfect hail of high explosive falling round him.   I spoke to him and he told me that nothing could be done.   He refused all offers of help from my artillerymen, who were unarmed, and sent them off to get through if they could.   His magnificent bearing, dauntless courage, and determination to carry on to the end moved one's emotion."   It is on record that this band steadfastly refused to surrender and fought to the last man, Anderson-Morshead himself being killed. and my old friend, Radford, then Regimental Sergeant-Major, being wounded and taken captive.

Another glimpse is of the 5th Battery R.F.A. who were supporting the right brigade.   They were luckily able to keep up a steady rate of fire " during what seemed an interminable night. Lieutenant Large and 2nd Lieutenant Button frequently took their places with the gunners in the reliefs, while Captain Massey kept moving from pit to pit and dug-out to dug-out and then to the detached sections, encouraging the detachments and telephonists and reminding them of the splendid traditions of the Royal Regiment.

" By about 5 a.m. No. 4 gun had been put out of action owing to a shell splinter tearing up the guides.   The detachment was withdrawn and sent in to reinforce the other detachments.

" The strain on all concerned was terrific, but at last at about 6.45 the enemy's barrage lifted clear of the position.   Instead, however, of the expected respite, large numbers of German infantry and gunners came into view less than two hundred yards from the battery position. A few rounds were fired at point-blank range, but it was then reported that Germans were coming up in rear. There was nothing left but to resort to rifles and the Lewis guns. Captain Massey, realising the situation a little earlier, had called for volunteers and pushed off with four gunners and a Lewis gun to a small eminence to the eastward in an endeavour to protect the flank. Nothing more has been heard of Captain Massey and his men. Lieutenant Large, although wounded in the foot, took the other Lewis gun, 2nd Lieutenant Button, after having destroyed all maps, papers, and records, was last seen moving off with a rifle to assist Captain Massey. The remainder of the battery fought to the last with their rifles till overwhelmed by sheer weight of numbers.

" Only three gunners, who were unarmed and were ordered to retire, and one with a rifle who fought his way out, survived. Of the two F.O.O.'s, 2nd Lieutenant C. Counsell and 2nd Lieutenant H. Reakes, and their telephonists nothing was heard again."

Both these epics were officially recognised, and the two units had the honour of being cited in French Army Orders and awarded the Croix de Guerre.

The third is at once the most tragic and the most surprising. The 2nd Northamptonshire Regiment under the command of Colonel Buckle had been the front line battalion of the 24th Brigade, and the C.O. had been reported " Missing, believed killed." His old father visited the spot after the Armistice. He not only found his son's grave close to the dug-out which had been his battalion headquarters, on

each side of him a German, but also his last message
still pinned to the dug-out wall ! This had been
written just before the attack. It reads :

"All Platoon Commanders will remain with
their platoons and ensure that the trenches are
manned immediately the bombardment lifts aaa
Send short situation wire every half-hour aaa No
short bombardment can possibly cut our wire and
if sentries are alert it cannot be cut by hand aaa.
If they try it shoot the devils aaa.
                    "C. G. BUCKLE, Lieut.-Col."

Equally this was the most disastrous battle on
the Western Front for the British troops engaged.
In no other did formations suffer such destruction.
The 8th Division was wiped out, in the strict sense
of the word. Among the infantry rank and file
the casualties amounted in every battalion to 550,
in some to a far higher figure. Not one infantry
commanding officer or adjutant survived, and the
company commanders could be counted on the
fingers of two hands. The losses of the three
regiments of the 23rd Brigade speak for themselves :

	Lt.-Col.	Maj.	Adjt.	Capt. or Co. Cdrs.	Lt.	2nd Lt.	O.R.
2nd Devonshire .	1	1	1	7	5	14	552
2nd W. Yorkshire	1	1	1	2	3	14	555
2nd Middlesex .	1	1	1	4	2	18	578

Remember these were weak battalions before the
attack.

Nor were the actual fighting troops the only sufferers, and for once the hand of war fell almost as heavily on staffs and rearward services. One infantry brigadier was gassed, another killed. The field ambulances, the motor and horse transport of the supply train all suffered in proportion. The total ration strength of the Division during the time that the transport was at La Loge Turbanne was 1500 ! The battle, following those of the Somme and Villers Bretonneux, brought the grand total of casualties suffered by the 8th Division in under two months to over 17,000—ample justification surely for our claiming with a certain mournful pride to have been the unluckiest division in France.

The more cheerful part of the story remains to tell, and the totals of casualties were, we were later relieved to learn, somewhat offset by the fact that a high proportion were prisoners. The German superiority in numbers enabled them to envelop our more scattered troops and round them up almost at will. Many friends of mine whom I had thought dead and gone have turned up as the years have passed to tell me they were taken in the trench system itself or trapped in some village, wood, or farmhouse.

Lastly, for all its violence and its sustained, intensive action, the battle was a reversion to a cleaner and more wholesome type of warfare. It was fought in fine weather and in lovely country, and largely with mobile weapons such as rifles and machine-guns, instead of in crabbed trench systems where men, leg-shackled by the clinging mud, were battered into the filth and ooze by high explosives.

When two months later King George V. conferred

the Victoria Cross on General Grogan for his great gallantry in the action, I decorated my note of congratulation with a little sketch of him mounted on Sandy on the Treslon Ridge.   In his reply, which I still cherish, he said he would keep my letter " as a personal remembrance of the very strenuous and I hope cheery times which we passed together on the Aisne and the Marne."   That seems to describe that fortnight more accurately than might be imagined.

THE GERMAN SIDE

By

*MAJOR-GENERAL A. D. VON UNRUH,
Chief of the General Staff, 4th
Reserve Corps (Corps von Conta)*

THE GERMAN ATTACK

From May 25 to June 1, 1918

THE great offensive on the Somme which had begun on March 21 ended, so far as the Army Corps von Conta was concerned, with the occupation of Noyon on March 27. We of the General Staff went into rest billets at Vervins, though there was no question of rest for us, as we were to be entrusted with the preparation of a fresh offensive.

General Ludendorff was anxious to transfer the victorious operations begun on the Somme to another front, but his first plan to attack in Flanders proved impracticable owing to the strength of the English forces and their large reserves. The position in the sectors on either side of Rheims was very different. Here the enemy was not only weaker in line, but he had no reserves. The front opposite our Seventh Army on the Chemin des Dames was particularly sparsely garrisoned, probably owing to the natural strength of the position. The question was, Had our General Staff confidence that they could overcome these natural obstacles, or was the country over which any advance would have to be made, too difficult ?   Obviously the attack would have to be prepared most carefully and could not hope to succeed unless it took the enemy by surprise. The morale and fighting spirit of the troops was excellent.   There was no doubt about their quality. Unfortunately the numbers available, especially in heavy artillery, enabled us only to contemplate an offensive on a comparatively narrow frontage. Still, having weighed the pros and cons, General Ludendorff and Field-Marshal von Hindenburg decided to attack.   Such action would at least compel the enemy to fight, and thereby prevent him surprising us at an unwelcome spot.

The Seventh Army, led by Lieut.-General von Böhn, was entrusted with the responsibility of carrying out this decision. Headquarters Staffs and reliable attacking divisions which had already distinguished themselves on the Somme were now withdrawn, made up to strength with reserves, reinstructed behind the lines, and gradually placed in the rear of the Seventh Army.   Here they enjoyed a well-earned rest in the quiet French villages, and soon recovered from their experiences in earlier battles.   The line held by the Seventh Army ran north of the Chemin des Dames and north of the Aisne, as far as the district north of the Rheims fortress.   The front of attack was approximately Coucy le Château-Juvincourt to north of Loivre.   The right flank was covered by the group of General von François, then followed the attacking corps of Generals von Larisch, Wichura, Winckler, von Conta, and Graf von Schmettow. Alongside towards the east was the First Army opposite Rheims.

On April 25 I was summoned to the Chief of the General Staff, Seventh Army, who instructed me to reconnoitre the sector Neuville-Chermisy-Bouconville-Corbeny and to ascertain whether an attack against the heights of the Chemin des Dames and the Winterberg (Californie Plateau) was a practical proposition. I was told to examine, on the basis of my experience as former chief of staff of the Carpathian Corps, if and by what means such an attack could successfully be developed. I was asked to examine the problem in particular detail so far as Hurtebise farm and the Winterberg were concerned. Did I think it possible for the Winterberg to be stormed? How was the attack to be planned and how many troops would be needed?

This was a task surely to delight the heart of any soldier. I asked to be allowed two or three days in which to do it, and this was granted. Walking alone, I spent the ensuing days and nights going in scrupulous detail over the sector and noting with satisfaction the nature of the ground and some not inconsiderable disadvantages of the position from the point of view of the defence. When I came close to the enemy front line on the Aisne at night I was both hailed and shot at by the English. They even offered me cigarettes, but I did not trust this friendly gesture and preferred to keep still and rely upon the cover of the darkness whenever my presence was detected. This personal reconnaissance enabled me easily to get an exact idea of the front line and all its difficulties, and I was further helped by the knowledge, experience, and observations of our front-line patrol leaders and scouts. As a result I reached the conclusion that the crossing of the swampy ground and the waterway of the Aisne should not of itself present any special difficulties. It was only a question of having sufficient bridging apparatus to hand and of effectively destroying the wire obstacles and deep dug-outs with minen-werfers and trench-mortars. The conditions for the latter looked very favourable.

At first sight the heights of the Chemin des Dames and the Winterberg seemed to be dead. There were no signs of life. I saw only the white chalk crest of the Winterberg, so dazzling in the sunshine that it looked as if covered with snow—a fact which had probably given the name to the hill on and around which so much blood had flowed in the preceding years of the war. It seemed to tower over the whole district and with its steep slopes, close pitted with hundred-thousand holes of bomb, grenade, and shell, and barred by formidable wire-entanglements, looked to be impregnable. Yet it had on an earlier occasion been stormed by German troops and they none other than my old regiment, the Infantry Regiment von Courbière (2 Posen), No. 19, who regarded the action as their greatest achievement of the war. Unfortunately we had not held the hill, and fierce attacks, carried out with a colossal expenditure of ammunition, had transferred the possession of this blood-soaked piece of high ground back to the French.

But observing it and the Chemin des Dames with a good pair of glasses for hours on end and day after day, it was quite evident that both positions were very much alive. Orderlies could be seen coming and going. Here and there was an occupied observation post, and now and then steel helmets could be spotted moving along a trench. The trenches and wire looked to have been strengthened. It was not difficult for a trained observer to locate the enemy's strong points and indeed to trace the scheme on which the defences were based. The old trenches and shell-craters on the bald forward slopes which had suffered most from our artillery fire were clearly seen to be filled with barbed wire, but the numerous gulleys and ravines seemed to hold much shell-torn undergrowth which was likely to afford excellent cover. Our F.O.O.'s, with whom I kept in close touch, were unable to bring these under full observation, though it was concluded that in many of them the English would have constructed carefully prepared support points. These would therefore be fatal to any attack which was not supported by the most exact artillery preparation. Equally, care had to be taken of the flanks, particularly to the east of the Winter-berg, and these would have to be secured at the outset.

The command of the sector from which it was proposed to attack was in position warfare in the hands of Cavalry-General Graf Eberhard von Schmettow. He was intimately acquainted with the terrors of the Winterberg and all the conditions surrounding it, and it was to him that I reported on completion of my reconnaissance, at the same time telephoning my return to Head-quarters Seventh Army. Later I went to Army Headquarters to find there H.I.H. The Crown Prince and General Graf von Schulenburg, to whom I outlined the conclusions I had reached. I told them I considered an attack possible without great loss if carried out on the widest practicable front and supported by strong artillery fire. The main weight of the artillery preparation would have to be concentrated on all the prominent points and open spaces so as to sweep a way for the assault. The gulleys and other places where direct observation was not possible would be rendered untenable by gas and by a barrage of minenwerfers and trench-mortars. On the strength of my report I received instructions on April 30 to work out a draft plan of attack in the sector Neuville-Chermisy-Bouconville-Corbeny against the Chemin des Dames and the Winterberg, as the Corps von Conta had been given the honour of carrying out the offensive on this formidable bastion.

Preparations for the attack along the whole front were in the hands of Seventh Army Headquarters. They determined the boundaries and objectives of the attacking brigades, made preparations for taking up positions, saw to the siting of battery positions for all the thousands of light, medium, and heavy guns which would swell the barrage, and laid down their lines of fire. Air reconnaissance had to be continued, and the whole front to be covered systematically with a network of telephone wires for all types of weapons. Vast quantities of ammunition, both H.E. and gas shells, had to be brought up and stacked in the battery positions. Trench-mortar ammunition and S.A.A. had to be taken forward and hidden away in readiness.

Surprise was the chief factor. Therefore no more aeroplanes than before had to be seen, no other batteries than those in the old positions were to fire. As the enemy also kept a check of the ammunition expended daily there was to be no increase in firing. All movement by daytime was forbidden, as also were all individual reconnaissances carried out by officers where they might be seen by the English. The English were to be given the impression that absolute peace and quiet reigned in our lines, and that it was out of the question that an attack was being prepared.

The Army Corps and Divisional Commanders also had a strenuous time. Not only had every detail to be worked out, but the whole of the preparations had to be ready by the appointed hour, and then carried out to schedule with the precision of a gala performance at a theatre.

Every contingency that might happen in the meantime had to be anticipated and counter-measures worked out. Corps headquarters was still far in the rear, and this did not tend to make the preparations any less difficult. Eagerness in patrolling was conspicuous, so that special officers' posts had to be set up to warn troops and prevent movements by daylight. The Corps von Conta was allotted a front of attack six miles in width, with three divisions in the first line, two divisions in the second, and one division in the third. As this sector was the critical point of the whole offensive, it was exceptionally well equipped, although not quite on the scale of the St. Quentin attack. Each division had three infantry regiments, two heavy artillery regiments, trench-mortars, pioneers with bridge trains, signallers, and everything necessary for the attack, for bringing up supplies and sending back wounded and prisoners. The Corps had in addition its own artillery for counter-battery work and destroying special support points. We had about eighty pieces of ordnance for every thousand yards of attacking front. This vast collection of guns was to be employed as one unit both for the preparation and for carrying out the actual attack—that is, for the barrage covering the infantry and either destroying every living thing in its path or driving the defenders into their dug-outs. It was important that the infantry should meet with no appreciable opposition, as their orders would be only to crush the last flickers of resistance and to push on without delay. Each division received its exact plan of attack and individual orders, and in their turn passed on instructions to their regiments and battalions. Each piece of the attack was worked out on a map with the commanders and the General Staff officers. Each subordinate commander had his sketch of the attack. He had to know exactly what was required of him on the day of the attack, what difficulties might arise, and how they were to be overcome. The same careful preparations were made with the artillery, air force, pioneers, bridge-trains, trench-mortar and machine-gun units, with the flame-thrower, and with the medical and supply sections. The barrage presented much difficulty. This death-dealing girdle of fire had to be put down slowly minute by minute so as to destroy all life, or send the enemy into cover, and yet not delay the advancing troops for one moment. The great danger was that it would advance too quickly for the infantry to follow, so that the enemy would be able to rush from cover and put up fight. In view of the deeply-cleft spurs of the shattered Chemin des Dames-Winterberg district, this problem was a particularly difficult one.

Finally, on May 20 the Corps von Conta received orders to take over their sector of the front, and Headquarters moved up to Château Marchais. The divisions also took up their positions. The last stage of the preparations began and was considerably helped by the plentiful cover the district afforded, woods and hills to the north of the Aisne valley screening them from English observation.

In the Aisne valley, on the other hand, work could only proceed by night. All possible cover was utilised for the secret concentration of troops. The movement of new divisions and supply work could only be carried out by night. Bivouac fires by night were forbidden. Horses were not allowed out of the woods.

On May 21, General Ludendorff called together the chiefs of staff and discussed with them the final measures for the coming attack, which was to be launched on May 27. The Corps von Conta was to storm the Chemin des Dames-Winterberg and push forward across the Aisne Canal, across the Vesle on both sides of Fismes, and halt on the heights to the south of the Vesle where a new line would be established.

By that time, General Ludendorff thought, the attacking troops would be exhausted. He would be satisfied with this objective and then resume the offensive at another point. Accordingly, after their barrage had reached the farthest range, the heavy artillery allotted to us instead of taking up a more forward position were to be withdrawn at once for service elsewhere,

Ludendorff ended by asking whether any of us had any questions to put.

I asked whether, if the attack went according to plan, we could not push on to the Marne. Ludendorff asked when I thought we should have reached the objectives south of the Vesle, to which I replied : " We shall reach the Vesle on the evening of the first day and the objective on the morning of the second day." Ludendorff reminded me that it was twelve miles to the Vesle, and " how could I be so optimistic ? " I answered that our preparations were so thorough that if the information of their weakness in numbers was correct, we should overrun the English. Ludendorff's opinion was that his information was absolutely reliable. We were actually up against a single English corps of four divisions, without reserves. He admitted it would be very welcome if my optimism were justified, but in spite of it he did not intend to go beyond the Vesle.

My colleagues were also convinced of the success of the offensive. We all had a definite feeling that it had been so well prepared that the enemy would be surprised and overrun.

The last few days were devoted to final improvements in the details of the attack and to troops and formations taking up their battle stations. Our greatest concern was lest the English should spot our movements and direct a destructive fire against our closely massed troops. Patrolling in No-Man's-Land was forbidden, so as not to have any of our men taken prisoner and run the risk of their giving away any information. The English could see or hear nothing. They might at the most have been suspicious because in their daily spells of firing they were lucky enough to blow up a few ammunition dumps.

It was a tense moment. We longed to open fire.

ASSAULT

As soon as darkness fell our artillery suddenly opened destructive fire along the front of the whole army and directed chiefly against the English battery positions and headquarters. The Headquarters of the 50th Divisional Commander had been traced by the telephone wires leading to it, which were shown up on the air photos. Indeed our airmen had done their work admirably and their photos gave us the reliable information upon which the whole action was based. The accuracy of our long-range fire, by destroying headquarters and cutting telephone communications, rendered any control in the organisation of defence impossible from the start.

At closer range the trench-mortars began to demolish the English wire-entanglements, and our storm troops manned their assault positions. The battle, in fact, had begun before the enemy had realised it. The element of surprise, most important factor in victory, had been preserved up to the last moment, and a feeling of relief passed through our lines. Fortunately for our peace of mind we did not at the time know that an over-eager patrol had been captured the previous evening!

At first the English artillery replied weakly and soon ceased fire entirely, overwhelmed by our gas and high-explosive barrage. At dawn the assault began with perfect synchronisation along the whole

front.   The English trenches were at once overrun, and on the left the prepared bridges were
thrown across the Aisne.   Here the 5th Guards
Division advanced against the huge rampart of the
Winterberg, while the 28th Division pushed forward
in grand style against Hurtebise farm.   On the
right the gallant 10th Division stormed the steep
slopes of the Chemin des Dames.   Our telephone
lines to the staff positions were working beautifully;
in fact our communications were as near perfect
as they could be, and everything was going forward
without a hitch.

The first reports to come in stated that our
troops had crossed the Aisne at all points, and as
soon as it became light the F.O.O.'s could everywhere watch the attackers going forward so that
no occasion arose to give counter-orders.   Although
at the beginning of the attack only the enemy's
headquarters,   batteries,   and   a   few   important
approach roads were kept under artillery fire, the
main weight of artillery had now turned on to the
barrage which preceded the advancing infantry
at pre-determined intervals.   Indeed the positions
of the troops were shown by the line of bursting
shells.   This barrage was put down by that splendid
artilleryman and ballistic expert, Colonel Bruch-
müller, affectionately nicknamed " Break-through
Miller " by his men.

The infantry effort was concentrated against
recognised obstacles, as little opposition was expected from the low ground and the hollows which
had been drenched with gas.   Against the onslaught
of three German divisions, which were quickly
followed by two others, it was humanly impossible

for the extended and surprised English troops to stand up, and to all the inquiries which came through from Army Headquarters and the Crown Prince, we could truthfully answer, " Attack is being carried out according to plan."

Our losses were remarkable small. The enemy had no time to resist. The English, who could usually be relied upon to hold out in shell-holes, firing to their last cartridge, were given no opportunity by the violence and activity of our combined artillery and trench-mortar fire to display their customary coolness. They were up against " force majeure," and, first blown out of their trenches and then surrounded, sentry-posts, Lewis-gun teams, and whole platoons saw that resistance was hopeless and were reluctantly obliged to surrender. Everywhere one could see groups stumbling down from the high ground to be taken prisoner by our waiting troops. The total taken swelled to large proportions. Enmity, it seemed, was forgotten as soon as the men became prisoners. On all sides we saw English and German troops gesticulating with each other in default of the spoken word. Cigarettes, bread, and flasks were being exchanged, and I noticed what I had before observed on the Eastern Front when thousands of Russians and Serbs had been taken, that enmity between soldiers only exists so long as the battle lasts. I noticed particularly that the English prisoners cheerfully saluted the Crown Prince when they marched past him, and many a cigarette was handed to them from his car.

Pioneer troops and labour units got to work on the heels of the advancing infantry to repair the shell-wrecked roads, especially those over the

Chemin des Dames. This repair work was of the first importance, enabling the guns, trench-mortars, ammunition supplies, and bridging-trains to go forward, without which the advance would have been held up. Other troops were busy unearthing shattered dug-outs in the search for English wounded. It was only our own artillery that followed the attack over the pontoon bridges and improvised roads, the guns that had been allotted to us leaving for duty elsewhere as soon as the barrage had ceased.

With the offensive developing strictly to plan, the Aisne Canal was reached shortly before midday and the crossing in force began as soon as the first bridging unit was ready. All this time the roads and villages in rear were kept under shell-fire from the Chemin des Dames. The Head-quarters of the 150th Brigade were duly taken and the Brigadier,[1] who fought heroically to organise a resistance, made prisoner. By evening we had reached the Vesle—in other words, in one day we had advanced nearly twelve miles. Yet it was reported that the English, both individually and in groups, had fought magnificently, sometimes submitting only when their weapons were literally torn from their hands. The fact was that, confident in the strength of their positions and in their efficiency and determination in defence, the English had been left without reserves ! Their local reserves could not be said to count. They were far too weak, and moreover we knew their positions and had subjected these to continuous shell-fire. I wondered at the time why the French were so long in sending

[1] *Brigadier-General H. C. Rees.*

support, for this only arrived after the 50th and 8th English Divisions had ceased to exist. Still, during the evening and night of May 27, there was some violent fighting around the crossing of the Vesle at Fismes. The English line here had been reinforced, but it was of little consequence as both our 10th and 28th Divisions had already succeeded in getting across the Vesle at several points, and the G.O.C. 36th Division reported that he would be in Fismes the next morning at the latest. Our General Staff were particularly anxious to take Fismes, which was a large and prosperous town, both on account of its strategic position and as a rationing and billeting centre.

By nightfall on May 27, therefore, all the objectives we had set ourselves had been attained. The first day of the offensive ended as we of the General Staff of von Conta had expected. There were no particular orders for the next day, for it was hoped that the heights south of the Vesle would be occupied by midday if not before, and these advance positions would then have to be organised at once for defence, as a French counter-attack would now have to be reckoned upon at any time. The main task of the Staff was therefore to see that the work of consolidation was pressed on with the utmost energy and dispatch, and road communications over the trench area rendered passable for vehicles carrying up all the material required by the troops. Through the night the pioneers and labour battalions worked uninterruptedly and stretcher-bearers searched the battlefield, chiefly for English wounded, and carried them to the field hospitals. The signallers meanwhile ran out new lines, those to the forward troops running across the shattered Hurtebise farm.

2nd Day.   May 28.

At dawn on May 28, Advance Corps Head-quarters moved up to the Winterberg. The shattered, blood-drenched battlefield was a grim sight, and we could clearly see it was so vast that the Winterberg alone would have needed a whole division to hold it. On the slopes columns came and went, and here and there vehicles sank up to their axles in shell-holes or into old dug-outs. A little below the summit there had once stood the village of Craonne, of which not a trace now remained except an English notice-board with the laconic information, "Here stood Craonne." It was through the one-time village that the road forward led, and along which telephone wires were laid, though, despite the greatest care, it was not possible to prevent them being frequently broken. But though communication with the advance troops broke down from time to time, there was no reason for alarm. The action would soon be brought to a triumphal end and then we should all go out for a rest. At least, that was how it appeared to us at that moment. We were to learn that things were not always what they seemed.

H.M. the Kaiser, the Crown Prince, Field-Marshal von Hindenburg, and General von Böhn arrived at the Winterberg about midday, when General von Conta was able to report that all objectives south of the Vesle had been gained. Indeed I was explaining the new position in detail to H.I.M. when the Chief of the Army General

Staff came on the telephone and gave the order from the German High Command, " Pursuit to be continued at once. Forward to the Marne ! " This was at 2.45 p.m., and the message was followed up by a lengthy Army Order indicating new objectives and lines of attack. The Kaiser dispatched me immediately to the front to convey his thanks to the troops and their commanders, and to give orders on the spot for a rapid prosecution of the offensive.

Meanwhile, as soon as the positions aimed at had been obtained, preparations were made for consolidating the new line in accordance with orders, and the troops tried to get what rest they could. The Corps von Conta was well in advance of its neighbours. To the left of us the Corps von Schmettow had met with a strong resistance and was still held up. Our 5th Guards Division, however, on the left flank, had partly changed direction towards the east, and had assisted by this turning movement the advance of von Schmettow's men against the remains of the English 8th, 21st, and 25th Divisions. In other directions the 10th Infantry Division were in position south-west of Fismes, and the 28th Division to the south-east. The 36th Division were concentrating in Fismes after clearing the heights along the Chemin des Dames ; the 231st were to the north of them and the 237th now striking south over the ridgeway.

Haste was necessary if the orders for immediate pursuit were to be carried into effect, since when once troops have been allowed to rest it is difficult to bring them again into rapid movement. There was no time for a corps operation order. It was a case for giving rapid individual instructions on the spot.

The streets of Fismes were crowded as those of a great city. Each individual battalion and company struggled to get a share for its own men of the abundant stores found there. There were enormous quantities of tinned food and preserves of all descriptions which our soldiers looked on as delicacies almost unheard-of. Articles of clothing, underlinen, and good English boots were seized upon with joy. Everywhere could be heard the astonishment of our less fortunate troops who were accustomed only to the monotonous if nourishing fare dished out by the field-kitchens. There were also plentiful supplies of alcohol and this was a more serious matter. There was a danger that it would slow up the momentum of the advance. The problem was therefore first to take charge of the captured stores and organise their distribution so that every unit got its share and yet ensure that excess was avoided ; and secondly to get the troops out of Fismes as quickly as possible.

I was abundantly grateful that no enemy bombing planes or alert batteries picked out the town as their target. Had they thought of doing so, or been in a position to do so, our losses could not but have been terrible. Such an experience I had had after the capture of Noyon in March, and I knew only too well the ghastly damage that shell-fire could cause to a congested area. At Fismes, mercifully, there was perfect tranquillity. Not a shell or a bomb fell. The French and English left us alone.

I then rode out towards the left flank where the high ground held the key to our further advance.

On the heights south-east of Fismes I found General Prince von Buchau issuing orders for consolidating his position, and gave him instructions that his division should forthwith attack the heights of Cierges via Courville-Coulognes. Orders were clear that there was no waiting to link up with other divisions in a co-ordinated advance, but divisions were to vie with each other in reaching the Marne as quickly as possible. With a cheer for the commander-in-chief, the gallant G.O.C. set his men on the move. As soon as they met with resistance he took his place at their head, and it was there that he met his death shortly afterwards. The 36th Division moved off as quickly and began penetrating beyond Fismes to the south.

Owing to the unavoidable delay before I could reach them, the 10th Division on the right flank had already halted and the men were resting after two days of continuous activity. The Divisional Commander with his chief of staff being already on his way to reconnoitre the new position, I drove the Regimental (Brigade) Commanders to the front and gave them their new objectives direct.

We had thus three divisions in the front line and the 5th Guards Division on our left flank, prepared to form a defensive flank or to strengthen the front of the 28th Division on the left if this open flank became seriously threatened, or was temporarily held up, as repeatedly happened. In this respect they performed excellent service.

The pause in the advance on both sides of Fismes, short though it had been, had given the enemy an opportunity to settle down and rally to resist our advance. We now met with resistance all along the front, and this had to be overcome before the line went forward. Moreover, the moving up of guns and ammunition now took longer, so that the nett gain of the second day of the offensive was far less than that of the first. By afternoon the line had only gone forward about two to three miles. The 28th Division took Courville, where again they captured large stores.

The Higher Command was not satisfied with this rate of progress, and orders were issued for an accelerated rate of pursuit on the following day, May 29. The infantry in the firing-line were to be accompanied everywhere by trench-mortars and field-guns which were to blast away opposition by directly observed fire. Staff as well as pioneers worked all night to make the roads passable and reinforcements of labour troops were rushed up. The engineers built temporary bridges and repaired those destroyed by the retreating English, so that guns, ammunition, and bridging equipment could be pushed forward. Order was restored in Fismes, and a strong staff posted there for administrative purposes. There also the Staff were billeted and passed a busy night. Otherwise all was quiet. No enemy aeroplanes or guns disturbed our all-night activities.

3rd Day. May 29.

Order having been restored behind the front, all attention was concentrated on the advance. The Marne was to be reached by May 30 at the latest.

The Corps von Conta marching off under orders of the Kaiser found little to bar their progress, which was well ahead of their neighbours' on either flank. The latter had begun to easy up before the pursuit orders had reached them, and accordingly took more time to get on the move again. Also enemy resistance on the flanks had stiffened, whereas the rapidity of our movement had prevented a similar organisation of defence in the centre. There were plenty of isolated hand-to-hand struggles, but these lacked any central direction and our superior numbers always turned them in our favour. The enemy were very skilful in the employment of machine-guns, but were without artillery, which was indeed already in our hands.

Although the English Corps had been left to hold their sector without any effective reserves, the French High Command, now that the catastrophe had happened, were not slow in bringing up heavy reinforcements to the line of the Marne. The resistance of these new forces was now encountered by the divisions of our Corps, with the 36th well ahead of the others. Checked for the first time in their victorious advance, our divisions began inquiring whether they were to halt and consolidate. French prisoners belonging to a number of divisions were brought in, and on being interrogated it was disclosed that they had been brought up in lorries and thrown into action before the main body of their formations had arrived in the theatre of operations. The order was accordingly given to continue the attack ; the Marne was to be reached as soon as possible. Though we took Fère-en-Tardenois and the heights to the north of Cierges and Cierges itself, the advance was materially slowed up by the French reinforcements, so that when, towards evening, Army Headquarters was asked whether the Marne crossing was to be forced, the answer was in the negative. The Marne was the objective of the Corps von Conta.

4th Day. May 30.

Our three divisions—10th, 36th, and 28th—in the front line were followed by the 231st behind the right flank, and the 5th Guards Division, still fighting towards the exposed left flank. On this day, when the Marne was to be reached, the enemy resistance had so stiffened that both the 231st and the 5th Guards had to be thrown into the attack. The former was placed between the 10th and 36th and given Château Thierry as its objective. The 10th were unable to make much headway because the neighbouring corps on their right hung back. Here continuous fighting impeded the advance considerably, but with the entry of the 231st into line, the 10th Division were able to assist in the protection of this flank and changed direction towards the west along its whole frontage. The situation was much the same on the left. There the 28th Division were held up owing to the difficulty experienced by von Schmettow's corps in keeping pace with us. Accordingly General von Conta on his own initiative prolonged his own corps front by taking over part of von Schmettow's sector with the 5th Guards Division. So with both flanks lagging behind, the Corps von Conta reached its objective, the Marne, in the evening with the 36th and part of the 231st Division, which had also been forced to follow the 10th Division in a westerly direction. The 28th Division spent the whole night in action in the great forest between Jaulgonne and Treloup. Our corps head-quarters spent the night at Dravegny with the 78th Reserve Division, and there received the news of the great capture of stores at Fère-en-Tardenois, and particularly of an American dump of almost fantastic proportions. This gave us our first impression of the American Army. We realised with what prodigious resources of material the U.S. troops were supported. We were destined not long afterwards to make the acquaintance of fresh American troops in action west of Château Thierry and in the Bois de Belleau. There I was to see young regiments coming on in masses, exactly the same as earlier in the war I had seen the Russians advance. The difference was that unlike the Russians, the Americans were supported by a volume of fire we could never have concentrated owing to our diminished resources in ammunition.

That gigantic American dump was a disappointment. There was little we could do with the enormous quantity of valuable stores it contained. We certainly re-equipped our whole forces in the area with wagons, wagon-parts, horseshoes, harness, tools, and other necessaries, but we had ruefully to abandon the huge supply of ammunition with which we might have been able to win a large-scale battle. We could not carry it away because we had not the transport. The question of supply had indeed become acute. We had no mechanised columns, and our railhead was far away in rear. Besides, there remained the barrier of the Chemin des Dames to overcome. Our four-legged friends therefore went through a very rough time, but it was some consolation to be able to feed them well on captured oats ! Yet the excellent liaison between the General Staff and the Quartermaster-General's branch resulted in our resources being handled so well that our troops never went short, although we had to exercise the strictest economy in our expenditure of ammunition, an economy which must inevitably militate against the success of any action.

5th Day.   May 31.

Early on the next morning (May 31) the 28th Division and the remains of the 231st Division also came on to the line of the river, the latter against Château Thierry which they had still to take. The 28th took a well-earned spell of rest in the thick forest to the north of Passy. The weight of the 5th Guards Division had enabled the right division of von Schmettow's corps also to reach the Marne.

By this time the right flank was definitely the danger zone. The French resistance was steadily increasing. Indeed violent French counter-attacks had already begun. The 5th Guards Division was therefore withdrawn and transferred in support of the right behind the line held by the 197th and 10th Divisions, the former being taken over from von Winckler's corps. Our dispositions were now five divisions in line (197th, 10th, 36th, 231st, and 28th), with only the 5th Guards and the 237th behind the right flank. It was imperative for us to push forward and thereby assist von Winckler's men to advance. Our headquarters were accordingly moved nearer to this flank to Fère-en-Tardenois, where we at once became a target for enemy gunners.

Meanwhile a reconnaissance on our left flank showed me that von Schmettow's corps could not hope to advance much farther. The resistance from the south bank of the Marne had become too strong, and every attempt to make ground towards the east broke down under the heavy flanking fire it encountered. The only way out would be to cross the river and gain possession of the heights south of it, for by so doing, the ring around Rheims would be drawn closer. This would, however, be a dangerous move, for with the Marne in our rear and our communications leading over the rampart of the Chemin des Dames we should be particularly vulnerable to the strong French counterattacks which were now to be expected. Yet the only orders we received were to secure the bridgeheads by throwing weak detachments across the river. This also was a dangerous manœuvre which would only serve to draw on the enemy, and could only hope to succeed if carried out under direct observation and adequately protected by gun-fire. I had had experience of such tactics both at Bzura against the Russians and Semendria against the Serbs. In spite of all the precautions we might take, we were bound to lose men, as it would be a costly business to bring the detachments back across the river under fire. We quickly abandoned the project, deciding that now it would have to be all or nothing. We, at any rate, were ready to make a crossing in force, but neither orders nor permission to do so were received. The Marne front suddenly became quiet, and our attention and energies were transferred to the threatened right flank. Here the decision would be fought out. Though we told ourselves and our men, " On to Paris," we knew this was not to be.

6th Day. June 1.

The actions developing on the right steadily assumed the character of a major engagement. The 231st Division certainly succeeded in taking Château Thierry where they found black troops from Madagascar, hitherto unknown to us, hiding in cellars, and we also advanced a substantial distance farther to the right where the 237th were in line. We captured the Bois de Belleau, later to become a famous battle-ground of the Americans, and also Hautevesnes Bussières. But our casualties were increasing alarmingly ; ammunition was running short and the problem of supply, in view of the large demands, became more and more difficult. It became all too clear that actions so stubbornly contested and involving us in such formidable losses would never enable us to capture Paris. In truth the brilliant offensive had petered out. This unpleasant fact was quickly realised by the High Command and the order came from General Ludendorff for us to consolidate the positions we had reached.

The tremendous effect of modern fire is such that attack is only certain of success when made as a surprise against inferior forces unsupported by reserves, as was the position of the English in the Champagne. As soon as fresh and strong reserves arrive, the momentum of the attack must slow down, until a fresh blow is organised and delivered.

Given equality in troops, it is ultimately the number of weapons and the way they are employed that is the decisive factor.

The enemy failed particularly in the air, where they should have been able to work wonders. We first learned to estimate properly the value of this important new arm when later on an order from the High Command sent us over the Marne.

Despite the great defeat of the English on the Aisne, we carried away the impression that they did their duty. They fought well and their sacrifices in blood and in prisoners secure for their IXth Army Corps a place of honour in England's history of the Great War.

TWELVE DAYS ON THE SOMME

A Memoir of the Trenches, 1916

SIDNEY ROGERSON

Foreword by Jeremy Rogerson
Introduction by Malcolm Brown

ISBN 978-1-85367-680-2
Hardback
192 x 126 mm

For more information on our books, please visit
www.greenhillbooks.com, email sales@greenhillbooks.com
or telephone us within the UK on 020 8458 6314.   Or write to us at :
Greenhill Books, Lionel Leventhal Limited, Park House,
1 Russell Gardens, London NW11 9NN

Other Greenhill Books on World War I include:

DIARY OF A DEAD OFFICER
Being the Posthumous Papers of Arthur Graeme West
Arthur Graeme West
Introduction by Nigel Jones
ISBN 978-1-85367-729-8

SAGITTARIUS RISING
Cecil Lewis
ISBN 978-1-85367-718-2

DOG-FIGHT
Aerial Tactics of the Aces of World War I
Norman Franks
ISBN 978-1-85367-551-5

CHRONOLOGY OF THE GREAT WAR, 1914–1918
Edited by Lord Edward Gleichen
ISBN 978-1-85367-428-0

INFANTRY ATTACKS
Erwin Rommel
Introduction by Manfred Rommel
ISBN 978-1-85367-707-6

THE GREAT WAR
Field Marshal von Hindenburg
Abridged and Introduced by Charles Messenger
ISBN 978-1-85367-704-5

T. E. LAWRENCE IN WAR AND PEACE
Edited and Presented by Malcolm Brown
Foreword by Professor Michael Clarke
ISBN 978-1-85367-653-6